Fountain of Living Water

Fountain of Living Water

R. Shelton, BCTMB, NCLMT

Fountain of Living Water

Hardcover ISBN: 978-0-999-8586-5-3

First printing: 2022

Printed in the United States of America

Available Anywhere Books Are Sold

Library of Congress Catalog Card Number:

Paperback ISBN: 978-0-999-8586-4-6
E-Book: ISBN: 978-0-999-8586-6-0

There Are No Substitutes for Water

No Water, No Life

Without It We Suffer

By Day and By Night

For If We Should Lose It

It Will Cost Us Our Lives

So Drink Up, and Drink Deep

Of the Water of Life

Acknowledgements

Thank you, Lord, for gifting me with the ability to write and touch hearts the way you have touched mine. When I first started writing the previous book, *"Member Heal Thyself"* back in 2014, I thought that it was going to be a one-and-done type of thing. Never in my wildest dreams could I have imagined that you had more in store for my life than that. Nor could I have fathomed the lives these books will touch and in so many ways.

With each title, I am ever more humbled by your power and grace not only towards me but to every single one of your children. I am ever grateful to be a part of this work and only hope that I can in some small measure give others a peek at the wondrous depth of thy love for them in your plans for each one of our lives and for your active role in them as well.

I want to thank my husband again, who always is there for me. You are an everlasting example in my life of what heaven on earth is and can be. I look forward to the beautiful kingdom we are building and in which we will get to live.

I'm also ever grateful to my amazing clients and the sometimes very surprising depth of love and support for this work being done to help others too, being so understanding and dedicated to their own wellness.

And to Viannah, my amazing editor, who put the finishing touches on this book to make it shine, I am ever grateful for you catching my typos and smoothing things so that they read the way my heart wants the words to be understood.

Last but not least, I want to thank *you*, the reader. It takes courage to move forward in your life, to embrace the joy that God has for you. I hope you will see the amazing gift hidden amongst the pages of this book for you. It is one of hope and endurance. These times now are challenging to the very strongest among us. Stay strong and help lift those around you. If we all lift where we stand and stand together, that is how we will make it through.

Contents

Contents

Part I
FLOODS

A FLOOD IS A HIGH-WATER STAGE where water overflows it's natural or artificial banks onto normally dry land. It can happen in a lot of different places: your bathtub, kitchen sink, or even laundry room or out in the yard when you let the hose run too long. Sometimes due to earthquakes or manmade disasters, you might even have a dam break and flood everything downstream.

One fine spring day after book launching "Member Heal Thyself" I felt the need to take a notebook and a pen with me and drive to a very special place and wait for inspiration to strike. It was a beautiful day. Overcast but bright that morning. No one was around, just me and nature, so I opened the windows of my car, tilted my seat back a little, and looked up. The beautiful yellow blossoms of the Palo Verde tree I was parked under were intensified by the reflective light of the hidden sun against the bright green bark of the tree and the happy rolls of low grey clouds softly drifting above. I waited and waited for something to come to me. Nothing happened and I questioned my initial thought to come here. Then, finally, the thought and feeling came to my heart and mind, "Time to start the next book."

An example in nature of a flood would be a river inundating its floodplain. Uncontrollable floods likely to cause considerable damage and commonly result from excessive rainfall over brief periods of time, as for example, per

Brittannica.com, the floods in Paris in 1658 and 1910, Warsaw in 1861 and 1964, Frankfurt am Main in 1854 and 1930, and Rome 1530 and 1557.

I could relate to feeling inundated by a flooding wave of mixed emotions that came over me as I thought about how the first book had taken so long to write, the many challenges and difficulties I had experienced along the way. The gut wrenching sensations and emotions that ripped through my body as I had to relive horrible memories over and over again as I wrote and rewrote, edited and reedited until I thought I might lose my sanity. What more could I possibly write? Writer's block. This time I had no book title or cover picture to start from and not even a subject.

These previous examples are not the only things that can cause flooding to occur. Ice jams during spring are a big problem for people who live near them, storm surges overwhelm riverbanks and streets, and tsunamis devastate towns and foliage – just to name a few. And they don't just affect our planet; they also affect our own body.

With my first book I had absolutely no idea what I was doing or how to do them. I had been on my deathbed for more than five years with no end in sight and was somehow supposed to write a book? I couldn't sit up or even hold a pencil in my hand. I couldn't speak right or think straight. I was on my way out of this life – big time!

God had told those around me I would be healed completely and that I would be even better than I was before. And, as much as I *wanted* to believe that would *be*, the way *my body and mind* felt – like there was no recovery possible or even being attempted by it, I had *serious* doubts. I knew I couldn't comprehend much of anything but I wanted to try to at *least* have a mustard seed size of hope. But it was a real struggle for me to even feel if I had that much strength left in me, I was so beaten down. If he could accomplish this, I thought, it would *truly* be a miracle because nothing else was working. And, if you read "Member Heal Thyself," you *know*, I have *seen* miracles.

Wise builders make allowances for different types of earthly floods that are likely to happen when considering how to best use certain land, methods, and where to build bridges, to predict and control of floods. They think about the best types of materials to use to handle a variety of situations and how to best put everything together.

I didn't know it yet, but a wise builder had already made preparations in advance for just such flooding in my life that could withhold the depth of my grief and longing for my heavenly home. He had chosen the best materials and shored up the sides long before I ever came to the outer limits of my pain. He knew the strength of the waves that would come crashing into my life that could have completely decimated me left unchecked.

There are other, less scrupulous builders who do not take possible flood situations into account but just want to slap something together to get a quick payday, and you can tell the difference in how things turn out after a flood.

There's always some cleanup involved after any kind of flood, but the difference between having to replace an entire building or just some sheetrock and flooring can be a big financial and labor difference. Not to mention the builders' reputations that end up being destroyed or praised.

I would like to *stress* to you, lest you *mistake* the low number of times I refer to the medical industry's involvement in this book as *not* holding them in high esteem. They have helped me when I broke my back and faced being paralyzed. They were involved with my sister's cancer, and my mother's, and grandmother's and many other instances that I will not go into. I am immensely grateful for the medical industry. I don't always agree a hundred percent with some of the diagnosis and prescriptions I've been given and I have seen serious misdiagnoses too. No one is perfect, and no industry is either.

Understand *I* am *not* a medical doctor and cannot and do not prescribe, diagnose, or treat disease so I will not be covering that. I have *seen* enough people though, that have *forgotten* along the way that there *is* a way to be healthy/healthier by simple lifestyle choices that they either forgot or *never* learned. My intent is to educate in that area to help you *and* medicine do your jobs *better*.

Common natural programs are used indirectly to help in case of floods, conserve soil and forests, help slow down and absorb runoff from storms and large surges of water. Even in a normal yard, things like having grass or trees, bushes, and plants definitely help keep the soil in good condition. It also helps maximize water absorption because plants are really good at drinking up some of the water and slowing down the flow.

These natural program methods are great news if you love to garden or landscape. Growing fruits and vegetables, even grass and flowers, can help to maintain the soil's ability to absorb and hold water in case of rain or flooding and help minimize at least some of the damage. The same holds true within our own bodies. There are certain natural programs that we can do to increase the body's ability to use and store water in the proper balance. These things can also help to get rid of or shed an overabundance of water being stored in the body as well.

What I will share in the book is the milk *before* the meat. Just like having grass or other plants and trees in your yard help slow down flooding, this early spiritual, emotional, and physical knowledge you will receive is the early assist, prevention and aids, for during a flood or traumatic health incident to help absorb some of the brunt of the flooding. It helps eliminate some of the damage that could have been worse. And just as these plants continue to drink up the water, these resources I will share also continue to help absorb and repair in some measure the damage done by your personal flood(s) in life that medicine cannot reach or cover that are not their specialty, as they themselves intended.

We cover different areas but work together. As we have learned in life if you try to break a single stick it is easy to break it but put a whole big bundle of them together and they are virtually unbreakable. Medicine **plus** what *we* will cover in my books create the bundle. And if you are reading these books, you *probably* need a bundle, as did I. I've learned there is no one silver bullet to fix everything but that you need many things, overlapping, for the best solution for you. And each person's overlap area will be slightly different, some drastically, depending on need.

Something we will repeatedly touch on is the wellness triangle because it is so critically important to understand and use in our own self-healing journeys. At each of the points we have the physical aspect of the body, the mental and emotional aspect, and the spiritual. Each one affects the others, and if you change one it will affect the other two. This holds true for each point of the triangle.

With each aspect of the wellness triangle there are different types of flooding in our bodies. There is the physical internal flooding that can be created by any number of imbalances of nutrients, toxic chemicals in the environment and pollution, and outside influences that are beyond our control.

There may be mental or emotional internal flooding created by thoughts running beyond their normal borders, or emotions that have gotten a bit out of control caused by our experiences, the way we've trained ourselves to think, some of which are completely within our power to change and others which are not. Even so, in situations where we do not have so much power to change, leave, or whatever, we can still control what we think or choose to feel about something.

Last but not least, spiritual flooding can happen too, and we can experience this when there has been a spiritual drought in our lives for a time. In drought conditions, plants die off, leaving the land waste and desolate. The ground loses all ability to absorb and hold water and our spirits become the same – wasted and desolate. If even a small amount of spirituality comes along, we feel overwhelmed and inundated, easily flooding our metaphorical banks, and we are not able to retain it.

There are many ways we can experience both drought and flooding in our lives and there are as many ways to cause them as there are individuals who have walked this planet. Much like vegetation has profound effects upon the soil we don't even consciously realize, our spiritual practices also fertilize our souls in ways we are not aware of but are *vital* to the health of everything else in our system and internal planetary environment.

If we do not prepare for flooding with systems *already* in place for the times in life that unexpected flood events happen, we will also be overwhelmed entirely. Soil, land, and basic flood proofing infrastructures that are not ready, get completely wiped out. When we become shocked and surprised by a devastating flood – emotional or spiritual – and have no plan in place, it can literally kill us. If it does not physically kill us, it can figuratively maim and harm us for a very long time.

Having life habits and support systems already in place allow us to be able to deal with trauma and other events when they come along. It doesn't mean it will take away the flood event, and it doesn't mean we won't have to deal with the cleanup afterward. But there will be *less* damage, it won't last quite as *long*, and we won't feel quite as devastated because we will already have the mental realizations to deal with things we otherwise would not have been able to handle. And we'll be able to do it more effectively.

Floods are usually caused by things beyond our control. They and their causal events normally have nothing to do with us or who we are. They happen, and it's just one of the facts of life. Still, they can affect us in very big ways. We have to get through them, but how and when we do, have a large part to do with the way we think and, feel, and the things that we choose to do. Some floods are caused by manmade events and choices, and either way the effects are devastating. The cleanup process is going to be almost the same, but when these events are caused by other people violating basic human laws, we also have to include holding them accountable in whatever aspect is appropriate for the situation.

It is my hope that you will keep all these different aspects of floods and flooding in mind as we go through the following chapters relating to hydration and apply them to your own specific situation in life. Ponder on the different types of floods that may be holding you back in life – or wading through the aftermath of – as you go.

Fountain of Water of Life

Chapter 1
Adam

WE LIVE IN A WORLD THIRSTING for knowledge but never finding it. We see people drinking in knowledge that never quenches the soul. We live in a vast array of lights yet only see darkness masquerading as sunshine. Seeing clearly requires more than merely opening and *lifting* the eyelids. It means we must dig *deep* within our souls and not only be willing to see what lies within but also what lies are without. And in this world where we live, there are *many* lies.

Some lies in life and the world we live in are so finely woven into the very fiber of our being, our tradition, our lifestyle, even our perceptions that we don't recognize them. Others are so blatantly obvious and unhidden we could never possibly dream of denying them. Some things are so true we'd never dare hope to believe in them for they are in direct violation of what we've been taught is true for generations. Yet, regardless of the outcome, truth is truth.

And so we go on, pouring ourselves into empty vessels that can hold no water, spilling out precious life source onto the cold, hard, and parched ground like nothing matters. It drizzles out as if it had no business keeping us alive. It becomes, in a way, invisible because no one dares notice. And no one dares say anything, for they are spilling their life source out too.

The lifeless water – falling and wasted – is empty, and so nothing grows in its wake. This is the way it is, and people believe that this is the way it will always be and no one has tried to fix it and they act as if no one ever should. That is, until one man came along who *could*. He has the skills, and he's got the talent. He was a man who was more than man and a son of God. One who could not only fix broken vessels but one who could provide living water to all who thirst for it. He makes old things new, heals the broken heart, and sings songs of life eternal to the poor, down trodden soul.

Sons of man can become great and do and have done great things. However, sons of God can go on and change the world in such a way so that they are never the same again. And *this* son of God certainly did. He lived his mortal earthly life filled with love, truth, and wisdom. He fought against falsehoods, imperceptions, and deceit. The perfect example of how to live with the most joy possible was one gift he left us. Without this we would not know which way to go. And without him we would not know the way to turn to get back home.

There are so many voices shouting among the din to come this way or that. All the noise makes it difficult to know for sure who is right, and who is mostly correct or only a little correct. And some are not right at all but profess to be. So who do you listen to, or even for that matter, who do you believe?

Yet there is hope. For a righteous God sent his son as a beacon of light and hope for the world and if we follow in his way, we shall surely find joy beyond compare. We will find love beyond imagining. And we will find hope to see us through any trial or challenge we may pass. Maybe you are in a place where you don't yet or don't want to believe in him or what he has done for you. You can still learn from the concepts in this book and I hope that you will remember them. For me, I have seen too much to ever possibly deny now but there was a time when I didn't.

We may see differently when we don't fully understand his plan for us or our lives. The trials I have gone through in my life have been very heavy for me to bear. I did not understand the things I needed to when many of them happened to me, even though I had access to the information that could have helped me more. Things weren't explained correctly to me. The adults around me did the best they could with their limited understanding. But some of them either just did not know enough themselves and others of them flat out lied, deceived, and betrayed me.

As I am entering into the last third of my life, I realize that as I learn, there are more and more things that these people didn't know. Some of them maybe just didn't care to know or preferred to profess that they did not know. And no matter how much we think we may gain by creating different realities for ourselves or for others so we may gain advantage over them, it just never works out in the end. Justifications hurt others but the ones we make up to ourselves are the biggest deceptions of all and not only hurt ourselves, it hurts everyone around us.

We all do the best we can with what we have in each moment, but how much better would it be to start with the whole, complete script right from the start? It would be ideal but perhaps not completely realistic given the fallen nature of man. We know we cannot do more than the best we ourselves know how. Things have been removed from our traditions, our everyday lives. These are simple truths, that have completely changed what we understand about who God is, what we've done, and who we are.

This lack of true and simple information causes mankind great stumbling blocks. It affects how we treat others, how we see ourselves, and how we interact in the world. Truth that is missing leaves a huge hole in the floor of our respective house. We all walk around it like it's not even there, somehow not stepping or falling into it, yet never seeing it. The missing information contained in that space is a gaping aspect of life, and we are missing out on it. It's time we start noticing and wondering what's there. And it's time to start searching for what it is. As we do, we will be blessed not only with great knowledge, we will claim the blessings that have been withheld from our view.

As we fill in the gaps of the hole in our metaphorical floor of knowledge, we may find that there is a door leading somewhere really important. Or we might find a staircase or some other type of portal that can transport us to locations of even greater knowledge and wisdom. One of the two, knowledge or wisdom, are nice to have, but how much greater and more complete to have them both.

As we follow the stream upriver, we will find it being added in to a larger river and that to a great river of wisdom. The goal as we continue to travel upstream is to reach the head of the fountain. To drink from the purest part; that is where we will find truth in its purity. Mankind is fallible, try as we might, not to be. It is in our natures to make mistakes as we learn and grow. And they can be used to our great advantage if we learn to watch, listen, and pay attention to all things around us.

Once we can embrace errors as a part of our growth and discovery, the speed at which we increase in knowledge accelerates tremendously. When we learn to combine this with experience, this can – but is not guaranteed to – turn into wisdom. Wisdom teaches us how to use knowledge appropriately and correctly and when not to.

Like a small child learning to talk, for example, those children that try and are willing to receive improved pronunciation techniques will be able to speak more quickly and be understood by those around them. This results in lower levels of frustration for both the speaker and the hearer. The child is able to communicate their needs and the hearer is then able to meet those basic needs, whether it is receiving food to eat, being held and comforted, or taking a nap.

We must learn the basics correctly first. It is when we do not learn correctness that troubles ensue. The initial patterns, habits, and truth or perception of truth as we see it, understand it, or are taught it – establish the foundation of all future things that we learn. And that foundation can determine if you have a house that will stand or a house that will fall with the first trial that comes along.

Started badly, whether intentional or no, causes hiccups in our progress. And undoing improper beginnings can feel painful at first. As we are willing to go through the necessary changes, though, everything begins to feel better, work better, and be built more securely. Performance improves, we are better able to handle things, and everyone benefits. We see our lives change before our very eyes.

Since perceived truths are merely perceptions – a distorted view of what things really are – we have to be willing to first recognize it is possible that we not only have one or two of them floating around but likely *many* of them. And we have to realize that we are not forever condemned simply for having false perceptions. Many of them are not even our fault. They become our fault when we choose to remain in them. But remember, change is always possible, and it's never too late. And it is never too big or bad of a problem not to rectify it today.

The more I study and learn about everything and how it all interrelates and the more I dig deeper for knowledge and understanding, the more I realize information has been stolen and hidden from us all. It has surprised me more every day the vast number of falsehoods we have been fed about far too many things. Basic, simple truths are as essential to our joy as water is to life. At what point these things were removed I have yet to discover, but I am more and more curious to find out.

Truth has been taken and replaced in some cases with nothingness. In other situations, instead of fountains of water of knowledge we have been given a substitute that does not fill or satisfy us. We've been given to drink of it for so long, for so many generations now that no one remembers there used to be anything else.

There used to be something better. It was really quenching. Everything about it was life-affirming. And so we sweat and strain under the effort, believing we walk in truth and light when there is something better, just out of our reach. We've become so used to walking under the weight of it we've come to also believe it is weightless. In reality we merely walk in the shadows just outside of the light – not seeing, hearing, or feeling but believing that we do. It's what we've been taught. It's how we've been led astray. It has been just enough outside of truth to be devastating.

An effect like that cannot be reversed overnight when a whole nation has dwindled in unbelief. The results would be catastrophic. It would be too shocking to the soul and to the mind. The heart could not take so much betrayal revealed all at once. Once you begin to have the weight of untruth removed, you start to notice how much lighter you feel and it's shocking to realize how heavy your burdens have been.

Many times, in healing, pain is removed in layers. Much like an onion has layers that can be peeled back until the heart is revealed at the center. Our soul has layers of hurt, pain, and injury. As each layer is removed, time and care must be taken to prepare the emotions and nutritionally support the body to withstand the releasing process. Each layer holds tightly to its conforming shape, pressing around and protecting the core concept. When care is taken, these layers can be removed without causing the onion too much damage, if even very little or none.

If you just went straight for the core of the onion you would end up with a big mess! You'd have weepy onion juice stinging your eyes, burning your nose, causing you to flee, perhaps, before even getting to the heart of it at all. We must start small and with the outside layers, working inward and deeper until we arrive at the center of truth. I have found we get the best results when we take the right amount of time, alternating with supporting and strengthening the weak areas until everything is caught up with the stronger ones before moving to the next level of healing.

You are only as strong as your weakest area at any given time, just like a dam wall. Sometimes we may be mistaken, thinking we can just hurry ahead and strengthen up our stronger areas and that will compensate for or cover up the weak ones, maybe even thinking we can then forget about our weaknesses because everything around them seems strong. Then we can speed ahead at full steam, right? For a while it may appear that way but at some point, we will have to go all the way back and address that weakness. Not just the weak area but also everything it connects to and works with.

The relationships between these weak and stronger areas also have to be strengthened, hydrated, and nourished and then be reconnected. And then everything it's connected to must be adjusted and corrected to incorporate the changes that have been made. At that point you've had to do at least *double* the work to get to where you thought you were going when speeding full steam ahead and not addressing the weaknesses initially. We may only *think* it feels better to rush ahead but it usually does not benefit us in the long run.

Fountains can appear in our lives physically and metaphorically. They can put out the fires in our lives if we seek them out. They can cool the burns from the fire of our pains. Our hoping the fires will just go away is not enough to make them stop. Action must be taken if healing is to take place. Taking action can seem to be the scariest thing in the world to do when you're hurting, afraid, and don't know how to proceed.

Even in the darkest moments of pain there are fountains of healing nearby full of joy, renewed pleasure in life and living, and even increased sensitivity. Drinking deeply from this fountain can help us experience an outburst of positive emotions as we are restored to wholeness again. And it can be a *full* restoration.

Healing can help us move forward into new relationships we were once lacking and even move us into a new phase within our relationships as well. When we don't know the fountain can be found within us, our life can feel so empty, overwhelming, like it's not worth living, and more.

We may try to seek other substitutes, but they don't really fill us. Not really. We only feel full but not filled. It leaves us seeking more and more in the opposite direction. However, the true fountain is there that will fill us entirely and we can find it just by knowing where to look and how to apply it in our lives.

We must use our own buckets. Then we need to lower the buckets into the water. Pull them back up. If we are not exercising these basic few steps, we can never drink from the water below. It's right there and available, but you must first, see it. Then reach for it. If you do not drink of it, though, it will never do you any good. You can hold it in your hand, looking at it and still never drink a drop and die of thirst.

That is one of life's greatest tragedies. That is, to have a cure within reach and yet to never take it simply out of stubbornness or ignorance. We never know how long we have left in life. We don't know how much or how far our influence goes in the lives of others good or bad.

We find the fingerprints of hundreds of other people across the windows of our souls. This influences the lenses through which we view the world and our experiences in it. It also affects the way we see people's actions, personalities, and words.

We only see what we *want* to see, not everything that *is* actually, and only *what* is there. We are affected and influenced as well by the grudges we hold still and what we decide we *want* to believe about someone else. (How often is what we believe unjustly degrading others, elevating ourselves falsely in our own eyes or in the eyes of others or ourselves?) We also like to think that we can calm the raging sea within us by affecting influence on others and changing what is out of control outside of us, but that doesn't actually work.

The belief that we can have a sense of control within ourselves by controlling the events and actions of others would be a false perception of peace in our lives. We must conquer our own life storms within ourselves and only ourselves and then and only *then* will we find stillness in spite of what rages around us. And the world *does* rage. As the younger generation says these days, "The struggle is real."

The world entices you with its artificial lights, artificial flavors, and alternate realities. It tries to make you believe, convincingly, that these other realities are better than what you have now. And so, like a moth to the flame, it beckons you ever closer. You don't realize you become blind to what's happening in the peripheral edges of your awareness. Your senses become duller and duller with each flap of your wings, carrying you relentlessly closer to the bright burning light.

Do we truly know if the moth knows the difference between true light and artificial? Do we know the difference either? True light nourishes and enlightens. It heals. And it helps things to grow. But as we and the moth fly closer and closer to the fake light, we are burned and fall, lifeless, never to rise again. Even if the moth doesn't fall on first contact, it cannot resist the irresistible pull to return again and again; it is a deadly addiction. It is a dance with death.

The moth believes, perhaps not unlike ourselves, that what it seeks is light. It is seeking a way out of its darkest night. To be freed from the pain and fear, the blackness all around it. And so it returns. Over and over until it finally succumbs to this life-sucking light, it returns. The result is always the same.

What is the artificial light in life? What is it that burns and cankers the soul and body? It's a trick question, of course. There is no one single thing. There are as many different types and variations of false ideas as there are people. Each one of us is weakened and damaged by different things and diverse combinations of things. Some are influenced by genetics making us more susceptible. Others are worn down over time and repeated exposure.

So what is a person to do? Many of us are trying to walk the path of our lives without a map or compass the best that we can. When times are good and fun, we may feel like we don't need those tools, *but* it's when the storms arise that we notice how terribly lost we have become. We struggle to find anything to grab onto.

We reach out to find something to help us feel more stable and secure. And perhaps we don't realize when we're really holding onto the very thing for safety that would burn us the most. For it is so cleverly disguised as to make one believe it is harmless. It may even seem exciting. As it strips away our life force one layer at a time until we are too weak and it is too late to stop or turn around, we then find that we cannot remove ourselves on our own or in time.

A person must want help or nothing will matter or benefit them, in my experience. Perhaps this is the reason why we are told to ask first and then we will receive according to our faith (which is our ability to act) and diligence in the book of

Doctrine and Covenants 4:7. We must knock before the door will be opened unto us. Both of these phrases contain an action verb. It requires us to actively *do* something. Then comes the cause-and-effect portion where all the action happens.

If you *knock* (the cause), *then* something will happen (the effect): the door being opened before you. This will then require another action of you. You must step forward and pass through the doorway. This will continue on in a cause-and-effect format. You must keep acting in order to gain the benefit of each effect and see the cause of your previous action. And this is how we continue to progress and improve. This is how we obtain heavenly help to remove ourselves from the unnatural light to true light and life by asking and then doing.

The journey towards truth and healing (or hydrating) that we will be undertaking will be an attempt to help understand how and where we begin to do just that. How we acquire the help in the area we lack it, learn how to apply it liberally to ourselves and our present situation, and how to use it to advance to the next (better) level is key. As we achieve excellence in an area, we can reach out to help those who are also asking for enlightenment in that same area, making sure we have drunk from the correct fountain first. We show them where and whom to turn to.

We need the cooling, quenching waters to heal the burned parts of our souls. That is not something we can do for ourselves. We *can* point the people around us who are also searching to the fountain where the water is and teach them about how to apply and use it, though. It is our job, even our duty, to do so. It's not something to be forced on anyone. Not everyone wants healing. And not everyone is ready for healing yet. Some may never want it in this life!

All you can do is love the people who are not interested or ready and patiently wait for their cry for help. In the meantime, we all have plenty to work on within our own selves that keep us more than busy enough. We must continue to move forward and keep one eye out for those reaching out for help. And you will find them, sometimes in the oddest and most unexpected places.

We eventually meet ourselves on the path of our own lives when we are ready to start facing our own inner demons. There will be things we don't want to see, things we can't *stand* to see. Things we regret or that make us feel ashamed will be presented to our conscious minds to review and process. This is not a bad thing to experience or to feel. While it can be unpleasant for a short time, we must view it as a sign of our growth and development. We feel badly now about it because we realize an error was made. A lesson was learned. We grew from it and we most likely would not repeat it. It's the body's way of telling us that we've grown so much since then that we'd not ever want to go back to that.

Think of your horror over past experiences as a year-end review. I was really bad at, say, drawing, when I first started, and now I can paint a masterpiece. When you look back at your first drawings you might be disgusted and embarrassed at how bad you were then. But you never could have gotten to be great at painting masterpieces today without having gone through the difficult beginning. Learning *is* struggle. Growth and change can be painful. Once you learn something better, what you knew before will become distasteful.

Ever watch a baby chick hatch? It's fascinating. You absolutely *must not* help them as they do it or they will die. If you help them and they survive, they will be very sickly and weak and not live long. It will be a miserable life for the chick. If they don't go through the struggle to peck their way out of the egg shell themselves, they won't develop the determination to make it in life.

A chick will peck a little and then they tire and must rest a bit but then they peck away some more and more until they start to see more light. They keep resting and repeating until they are finally free of their prison shell. The struggle helps them develop more muscles and strength, so once they emerge they are able to move around more and improve and begin to find nourishment. It also helps them learn that they must keep trying and never give up! And no matter how difficult a trial seems, if they keep working at it, eventually they will succeed.

We are no different from these baby chicks in the respect of needing to work through our hardships so that we learn never to give up. We need struggles to make us stronger. We must become comfortable with being uncomfortable sometimes. It is in these places of discomfort that we learn how to shine, where we discover hidden talents, and where we can cleanse our souls. Discomfort helps move us further away from what we do not want in our lives. It pushes us closer to the divine within us.

We cannot remove what we do not see. And we cannot see what we are unwilling to acknowledge or accept. We have to look or there can be no improvement. There will be no increase in us or for us. And there will be no growth in the areas we want most. And so here we find ourselves on the precipice. We are on the edge of deciding if we will go forward or go back. If the choice is to go back in our progress, then there is no need to continue reading beyond this point and if that's the case – that's okay. Not everyone is ready to go forward yet. It doesn't change who you are or how valuable or worthy you are.

If you are ready to go forward, get ready for a fire hose of information compacted into a tiny amount of space, and read on. You will find layers of knowledge within these pages that can help you on your way. Put on your seat belt, keep your hands inside the boat, hang onto your oars, and get ready because you will be paddling upstream as you drink from the fountain of water, full of life.

On the next page, you will find a list of supplies you might like to have on hand for the rest of the book. Get a drink of water, take a little eye break from reading, and give your muscles a little stretch while you're at it.

You May Need/Want These Materials to Continue:

- Fountain of Living Water Wellness Journal or other notebook for notes and impressions
- Pen or pencil
- Highlighter (optional)
- Glass of water or other hydrating drink, like cucumber water in our booklet
- Breaks for time to mentally digest information, ideas and for homework activities, get up and move around

An impression is basically a thought or an idea that both resonates in the mind and connects to the heart. The heart organ is considered a second brain by the medical industry, interestingly enough. Per dictionary.com's definition, an *impression* is "a strong effect produced on the intellect, feelings, conscious, etc. and the first and immediate effect of an experience or perception upon the mind; a sensation. This is an effect produced by an agency or influence. It can also be a notion, remembrance, belief, etc., often of a vague or indistinct nature. And it is an image in the mind caused by something external to it."

It is important to understand exactly what an impression is before getting started on the rest of this chapter. It's essential to know what these words mean and how to use them, not just to get the most out of the book but also out of life.

The first step to understanding an impression is to pay attention to those small thoughts and feelings. They will be very small, quiet, and faint. Usually, it is the first thought but can also be followed by additional wandering ideas. A wandering mind allows space for consideration and a fertile soil for emerging concepts.

Don't be frustrated if you are having a difficult time staying focused. It is part of the neural process of learning. Give yourself time and space for this to happen and to let it run its course. If you only get through reading a single paragraph for the day or just one new sentence, that is still good progress. What's more important than what is on the page is what you're learning through your impressions and what you understand.

The next step is to take a moment to write down the thoughts and feelings coming to you. Write down the good, the bad, and the ugly things. There's a reason they're coming up and it's to get your attention. Maybe it's to make you aware of how you've been feeling about something. It could be a more conscious awareness of something you've been struggling with that needs attention.

A situation that needs to be addressed in some form or another may be presented to you through an impression. There may be a new concept you need to consider or a next step you need to try and take. Whatever you set your intention to find, whether it be what your next most important step is to heal or to find balance in your life, stay focused on that.

Whatever the impression, it is important to write it down. It helps us remember it later, we have it to refer back to when we do forget, and we can look back a year from now and see how much we have learned and grown. We think we can and will remember, but the truth is, the more you pay attention; you'll notice you'll be getting a lot more impressions and memory fades and is selective. As we grow, our thinking becomes elevated, and we easily can forget where we've really been.

We can become frustrated with the learning and growing process. Sometimes things just don't happen as quickly as we would like them to and as much as we don't like that, sometimes it is just much better for us if things take their natural time to heal or recover. We all hope for an instant miracle (wouldn't that be nice), but remember the phrase "good things come to those who wait." Having a record that accurately reflects how far we've come can not only help us while we are in the moment but it can help remind us that we have done more than we recall.

Having a written record is a visual reminder we have made a lot more progress than we realized. It can be easy to fall into the trap of beating ourselves up for not already being fully complete. Our lives and experiences are an ongoing project that lasts a lifetime. Having a written record helps keep us from being too hard on ourselves and allowing ourselves a bit more grace. And someday, maybe future generations can learn things from us and avoid certain pitfalls we've discovered along the way. Our story is not just for us. It also can help others. It can be helpful for our children, our grandchildren, or even people in our communities. It's about the journey, not the destination.

Another great feature to keeping our impressions written down in a wellness journal is that once we have them in one place we can come up with a strategy or game plan for how we want to apply the new things we learn in our daily life. We can refer back to it as often as needed and if we lose the paper our game plan was written on or if we want to take what we learned to the next level, we have everything we need to get started in our original record. Sometimes it's nice, too, to be able to remember what things we learned as new impressions come up.

Looking back on things we have overcome can help us to renew our desire to reconnect with our truest self and continue moving forward. The collective view of where we are heading is exciting and we see life improvements we'd never want to live without. We can also see patterns, habits, and possible projections of where we might be going next. It's a wonderful resource to have. Football players review previous game strategies and outcomes from their play books so they can play better against other teams' strategies in the next game. What we are doing with a wellness journal is much the same. You can't improve what you don't track.

Impressions can help bump us in the right direction to be able to face the terrifying events that change our trajectory. Tragedies don't have to change our direction forever. We are meant to heal ourselves. But we are never meant to do it all by ourselves. We still need help to get there. We are strengthened in numbers, just like a bundle of sticks when placed together is much harder to break than a single stick alone.

Build a support team you can depend on and each added person becomes another stick in your bundle, making you stronger. Especially if these individuals are also working on improving their wellness in similar ways as you, you'll find camaraderie, as well as understanding and hope when you need it most. And the rest is up to you and your creator. Keep going until you get to the end of where you want to go. Then start again on the next thing you want to work on.

How does one start anything? Do you simply *begin*? Do you make a plan first? And what about the size or scale of the project; does that affect how much planning comes into play? Starting a project comes easily for some and is extremely difficult for others. Sometimes the same people who are great at starting new projects struggle to finish what they started. And sometimes the ones who struggle to start can't seem to stop themselves from finishing up every last detail.

We all have different strengths and weaknesses, so find people that complement you but are not exactly the same as you. This is why family units working together work the best for support teams if you can, but not everyone is always ready to work together, and that's when you build an outside support team for yourself.

It would seem that the more moving parts you have in a plan, the more detailed and organized your plan would have to be. When a computer programmer wants to create a virtual world online they have to do a lot of planning. They have to create a computer program with all the code for the graphics, the characters, and the buildings.

There must be multiple perspectives as different people interact with the computer and other possible players in the game as well, which means a lot more planning and coding. It takes years and years of development, testing, and trial and error before a program is ready for use. There's also a period of time to work out the bugs before the actual launch of this new game experience "comes to life."

When writing a book, the process can be a bit more forgiving. You can either plan one out from the beginning to end or you can "fly by the seat of your pants" – as the phrase goes. You can throw bits of this together and parts of that and revise it, remolding it as you go along. Watch as it takes shape until it is finally finished. Both may end in a final finished product, but only one of them will have less chaos and clean-up along the way.

Not everyone works best with the first method, but sometimes that's because we are just not used to doing things a certain way. We were never taught the steps. And much like in dancing, there are steps to follow. Even if a style of dancing seems to look chaotic and completely freestyle, it is still following a certain set of rules and staying within certain parameters in order for it to look good.

No matter what process you use and no matter the project, there must always be a beginning, middle, and an end to all things. One example in our existence is that of birth, life, and death. In the business world you might have a product launch, sales, and discontinuation or close of business. In the entertainment industry you might see a famous movie star or a singer who gets "discovered," has a career, and then you see their final curtain call.

The oldest beginning passed down by man speaks of a physical darkness. This darkness was known to be on the face of the deep. What is the deep you might ask? The deep is the waters of this planet. We know the Spirit of God *moved* upon the face of the *waters*.

The word *moved* is a verb, an action word. He was actively doing something in relation to the water. He wasn't just casually looking at it. There wasn't a God merely *seeing* it. There was an action that took place. If God must take action to accomplish something, are we any greater than he that we do not need to take action in order to create or accomplish a task?

Something I have noticed for myself and in the lives of clients I work with consistently is a similar kind of darkness. Often when we start out on our healing journey it can feel very much like a physical darkness that is on the face of our deep. It's a kind of stagnation.

We lack knowledge, a higher perspective, additional light we didn't have before that has previously prevented us from being able to free ourselves from this stagnant grasp the past has on us. These *darknesses* and traumas that are in our deep do not need to stay there. We can bring light and knowledge to change it to light. As we do the things required, we become lighter and lighter.

The things that are in our personal deep can vary from one person to the next but a very common theme exists that I have witnessed and experienced, even in my own life. And that is that there seems to be a lot of broken pieces of ourselves drowning inside. Often, we do not know how to retrieve and fix them, which is why they are still broken and drowning within us. Everything our traumas have left behind within us is cluttered and disorganized.

We are so busy trying to survive with the remaining pieces, that's all we seem to have time and energy to do. Stomping at the fires of our personal chaos, we don't have time to look for a water pail or fire extinguisher.

We often don't realize there are firefighters in our very midst and they are ready to help us not only find the water we need but help us put out the burning flames. On our own, it can be difficult to know where to begin and just us by ourselves is not enough to put out those flames. We need help. The beauty of it is, we were never meant to do it alone! It doesn't *work* alone.

We need a master organizer in our life to help us make sense of it all. A master puzzler who can put all the pieces back together is necessary. A teacher, too, who can show us what it was supposed to be and what it still *can* be. With this help we can have a greater perspective of all the things we cannot or do not want to see ourselves in order to clear the first path through the trauma. You've heard the phrase "you can't see the forest for the trees" and it holds true for us being able to see our forests. We are too close to our own experiences and perceptions that we cannot see what all we are dealing with, let alone how to find the quickest, shortest, and safest way out.

The original organizer of this world – and of us – divided the waters under the firmament from the waters which were above the firmament. What exactly is *firmament*? It means "expansion." It denotes the space or expanse, like an arch, appearing immediately above us. Modern dictionaries define it as the sky or heavens, as in dictionary.com, as just one example. If God is powerful enough to separate the heavens from the water on this planet, he might just be powerful enough to help us also do the same for us and our unique situation.

Our deep waters can have the same thing done to them as were done to this planet, in the beginning. We can divide them or organize them into different categories; the light things and the heavy, broken things. There might be categories of the things we don't want to think about yet and the things we can handle dealing with at this time in our lives. Everything has layers and is divisible. You know the great thing about division? Smaller things are a lot lighter, a lot easier to deal with, and happen to be a lot smaller in scale.

All layers have a foundation upon which they are built. For this planet, the first layer was the waters. This is the first thing you must know when you start your own healing. Every strong, sturdy construction or building must begin with a sure, solid foundation. If it doesn't, it will fall. You are no different. You need a good solid one to start out with. How good is your foundation right now? Could it be better? Pay close attention, and I will point out the various ways this can be done.

When we start the process of organizing our deep waters or personal traumas, sometimes it can feel a bit like trying to catch and keep water in our bare hands without losing a drop. We may try to hang onto it, squeezing our fingers ever tighter, only to find it starting to leak right through. Once it slips away, we can't seem to get it back and the water leaks out faster and easier than ever. It falls and seeps into the ground or evaporates quickly into the air off the hot pavement, never even absorbed into something that could benefit from the water.

We may feel a sense of despair, loss, or disappointment in ourselves or in our ability (or lack thereof) to hold onto this life-giving resource. It seems like it should be such an easy thing to do, just hold some water. But not all our hands were created equally for this simple task. For some this may seem like an easy thing, and for others it is impossible.

We may not even realize we might have some factors working against us from the start. Perhaps our hands were already soaking wet or all our natural, protective oils were washed away before. Maybe our spiritual or emotional self is so starved there's not enough metaphorical fatness to our fingers, leaving wide openings for the water to trickle right out. Things like that can sneak up on you and catch you unaware while you've been busy surviving and trying to stomp out life fires.

Once we realize we're not holding our water or that we are lacking the ability to hold water we may feel like we want to give up. We might decide to just go do something else. Do *anything* else. Let's just pretend the task no longer exists! It can't be that important, right? I mean, we've got fires going on here and pieces being broken left and right. How important could it be? Maybe we decide to completely give up and wallow in despair and agony at our failure in this one simple task.

There is a third option to know about and that is to find out what is causing the problem and find a solution that will work to fix it. How important would *that* be to you?

It could save your life.

This one task could very well be the key to putting out all the fires of the soul and mending the broken pieces. And once they are mended and restored to new again, your vessel will hold all the water in the world again, and you will be filled.

Fountain of Water of Life

We can fall into the trap of the downward spiral if we opt for one of the first two options. We could continually beat ourselves up. We could never allow ourselves to be restored to wholeness again. And that would be awful and not accomplish what you think it might. On the other hand, we could love ourselves and be self-forgiving as we go through our learning and healing processes. The difference between the two is as different as splattering the water on the ground and collecting it safely into one place together.

Many of us may find ourselves vacillating back and forth between these two places at various points in our lives. It's only natural when your confidence has been shattered and trust broken. It's hard to believe in yourself and your abilities when traumas have destroyed all your hopes and dreams. We may even discover how we feel about ourselves, and our progress and goals changing back and forth multiple times a day. The downward spiral is easy to fall into. It takes nothing to give in to its pull and takes mighty effort to resist.

What we can do is pull ourselves up by the boot straps, so to speak, and give ourselves allowances when they are due. We need to be as kind and gentle to ourselves as we would to a newborn babe. But we also need to be as encouraging to ourselves as we would be to a babe learning how to walk for the first time. They are so sweet and innocent, helpless and defenseless. These little angels from heaven rely on us for every little thing just to survive. Our hearts and souls are, at the very core, as deserving of just as much kindness and love.

As much as our spirit and emotions are deserving of our self-forgiveness and kindness to love and care for our hearts, our cells are just as dependent on us. They need us to give them pure, clean water so they can take care of our physical foundational needs. Our cells need water to carry out transportation services for things like nutrient delivery and trash pickup! This may not be something we really think about consciously, but it is essential to our happiness in life and, even more importantly, to our health.

If you don't have enough water, think about what happens. Medicine even supports this. Our nutrients don't get where they need to go. That steals your strength, energy, and, in time, your motivation. When the trash doesn't get picked up and removed, it starts to pile up and stink. Nobody likes that! You then get caught up in enough of a backlog of garbage that it seems impossible to ever be able to clean it up and soon things just start getting dropped wherever whenever because there's just no room or space for what needs to happen. This further restricts the transportation lines. They can slow down and finally stop.

The immune system, as per the medical industry again, needs a clean, fast highway to travel through to get to the cells. Think of your immune system like the ambulance or fire truck. When they need to come through on their way to an emergency, everyone pulls over out of the way so they can get where they need to go safely themselves – and in a hurry, if required. They monitor and protect us from foreign invaders and harmful bacteria that can make us sick or die.

Our nerves and brain need water to communicate and relay information like our mail or phones need pathways to help know how everything is running. It sends calls for help when something is wrong or broken. These are just a very small number of things for which we need proper hydration. When we are not well watered, it compounds all other problems more and more.

What's the solution? Love yourself more. Start with the little things first. These are usually easier to do too. As you get better at them, you'll gradually become more confident. Once you begin to feel your confidence growing, you'll naturally tackle the larger self-love activities until you are finally filled to overflowing with compassion. You can't truly know how to love someone else if you can't comprehend how to love yourself first. It all starts with water, as you can see.

If you don't know how to love yourself, drinking water and helping the body cleanse is an act of self-love. Taking good care of yourself first is an act of self-love, much like on an airplane when they tell you to first put on your oxygen mask before helping your child or the person next to you with theirs. You won't be any good to anyone else if you faint or pass out while trying to help someone else and you're not getting your own oxygen. The other person might not know how to do that for you. It might seem like the opposite is true that you should help others first and then yourself, but even the greatest among us took time for himself to retire and rest so he had the strength and resources to help others second. The spiritual reflects the physical and the physical reflects the spiritual. You have to help yourself first, just don't *only* help yourself or help yourself only all the time.

How do you know if you're dehydrated physically or spiritually? You can't change or improve something if it is not in your awareness. It also takes understanding of why something is so important to want to bring it into your awareness in the first place. Once you know and understand, you will be able to recognize the signs and symptoms and take appropriate steps to fix things.

So where do you start?

Let's remember we are not covering medical issues and start first with the knowledge of what dehydration is in all its forms and types. Since we are most familiar with the physical body and symptoms, we'll start with that, but know that you will always want to start with the spiritual when healing wherever possible. If you can't bring yourself to start on the spiritual water yet, that's okay; pick something and start.

Physical Symptoms of Dehydration

There are three levels of physical dehydration: mild, moderate, and severe. Severe dehydration requires *immediate emergency medical* attention. The person should be taken to the hospital right away. Other forms of dehydration are nothing to be trifled with, and steps should be taken soon to get mild and moderate dehydration under control before it gets to the stage where emergency care becomes required.

Mild Dehydration Symptoms:
2 – 3% of total body water is lost

- Chills
- Constipation
- Dark yellow urine
- Dry mucus membranes

- Flushed skin
- Headaches
- Less urine
- Loss of appetite
- Thirst
- Tiredness

Moderate Dehydration Symptoms:
5 – 6% of total body water is lost

- Cramps
- Extreme fatigue
- Faster breath
- Higher body temperature
- Increased heartbeat
- Little to no sweat
- Little to no urine
- Nausea
- Sunken eyes
- Tingling

SEVERE Dehydration Symptoms:
7 – 9% FLUID LOSS IS CRITICAL! EMERGENCY!

- Chest pain
- Coma
- Confusion
- Low blood pressure

- Mottled skin
- Muscle spasms
- No tears
- Rapid breath
- Rapid pulse
- Seizures
- Shriveled skin
- Vision problems

We know that thirst is an early sign of dehydration. Many of us believe we need a drink when we are thirsty. If we wait for this signal, we've waited too long and are already about two cups low on water. The lips start to crinkle and chap, although chapped lips can be indication of many other things, like issues with the lungs and spleen. No amount of lip balm or lip gloss will fix that.

Some issues associated with dehydration may be physical; some may be emotional or even spiritual. You can't just judge or diagnose someone, even yourself, by one single indicator – especially if you are looking at someone else. Their emotional condition, past experiences, allergies, and more can affect how things look and seem.

Start with helping yourself first before you do anything else. You can't help someone else if you are not in a better position than the person you might be trying to help. If someone has multiple symptoms, it may be that you can tell how dehydrated a person is and help get them drinking some water right away if that's what they need.

Usually, drinking water is enough to reverse physical dehydration in small amounts at a time. Adding electrolytes or a pinch of 'Real Salt' to your water can help or adding a tiny bit of honey to warm water. A syringe or teaspoon can be helpful when helping a baby or young child rehydrate. Avoid store bought sports drinks. These are filled with harmful sugar which can further dehydrate and give you diarrhea. Homemade fruit juice popsicles with a pinch of salt are a good option for kids who won't take fluids.

Seek professional help if you or someone you know is experiencing moderate or severe symptoms of dehydration. Get them to an urgent care, emergency room, or right into a doctor if you can. They are trained in how best to diagnose the situation accurately and take action as needed in the person's best interests in getting them rehydrated before it creates further complications.

There are a lot of books written on the subject of drinking water, of hydrating the body. And there are tons of products out there to increase your water absorption and journals to track your water intake. There are others telling you about dehydration and all the symptoms the body has that may make you feel like you are sick. People find that when they begin to hydrate, they start to feel better. They have more energy, and many physical and emotional symptoms they previously had seem to miraculously disappear.

Spiritual Dehydration Symptoms:

- Easily angered, quick tempered
- Lack of giving service, feeling spiritually drained. Growth creates overflow of love
- Lack of self-control, lose control over our flesh and appetites, addictions
- Lethargy towards spiritual things – due to spending time in other areas; suffering in personal relationships; feeling spiritual things are boring, unimportant, or it takes too much time
- Skewed judgment, not trusting in our higher power over our own judgment
- Tunnel vision, we only see ourselves and today
- Unwise choices, lack of enough engagement in spiritual matters

Take a minute and compare the physical and spiritual dehydration symptoms lists. Remember, some things can be signs and symptoms of something else entirely, so you can't just take one thing on the list and make a determination about someone else. Start with yourself. What similarities do you notice? Which physical and spiritual dehydration symptoms are you experiencing in your own personal life? Don't judge them or anyone else's list because we can easily judge falsely, not having all the information (our false judgments will fall back onto us). Just take note of the things you see about your own situation, and write them down for later so you can track your progress.

Chapter 2
Moses

HOW A BOOK BEGINS is never an easy story. This is why when you ask someone to tell a story, they always take a deep breath and pause. Trying to decide where your story begins and where your healing must start is no different in the beginning. One thing is certain though and once again, there must always be a beginning, middle, and end to all things. The oldest beginning speaks of a physical darkness that was on the face of the deep.

We know the Spirit of God moved upon the face of the waters. [1] Often, when we start out on our healing journey, it feels very much like a physical darkness that is on the face of our deep. I'm sure the same could be said to be true for Moses's origin story. When we look at his life from the outside, it is easy to see where the dark places might have been in his life. Where he might have struggled is easier to pick out than perhaps in our own tales.

What is in the deep of one's story can differ from one person to the next, even from our very own stories. As you recall from the previous chapter, a very common theme is that there are a lot of broken pieces of our lives – our identities – drowning in that deep. Often, we do not know how to retrieve them because everything is so cluttered and disorganized. It is difficult to know where to begin. Remember – the beauty is – we were *never* meant to do it alone!

Page 60

When we look at the broken pieces in Moses's story, it is easy to see that he needed a master organizer in his life in every aspect of the story. We see that God was not only aware of things going on but also putting the right people in place to help get Moses to where he needed to be in order to use him to bless not only Moses's life but the lives of many others who needed it.

Moses needed someone who could make sense of it all and put all the pieces back together in a much better way. And when the student was ready, the teacher appeared and was able to teach him what his life was supposed to be and what it was going to become. The original organizer divided the waters under the firmament from the waters which were above the firmament. [2] And he did the same thing with Moses's deep waters.

He divided and organized them into different categories; the light things and the heavy things. The things Moses didn't want to think about *yet* and the things he could handle dealing with *at that time* of his life. Everything was done in layers. And those layers had a foundation. It might have seemed to have started with a layer of sand but it had one and the sand was blown away to reveal a layer of stone.

When we start the process of organizing our deep waters or personal trauma, we remember the analogy of trying to catch and keep water in our bare hands. When we try to hang onto it, we find it slipping away between our fingers and not getting it back. We can choose to work through that sense of despair and disappointment in ourselves, our ability (or rather our lack of ability) to do what should seem such a simple task.

Even though we might want to give up and go do something else, pretending the task no longer exists is just not the answer, at least not permanently. That downward spiral is always waiting for us so conveniently close by, waiting for us to start beating ourselves up instead of being loving and forgiving during our learning and healing processes. It's usually a good indicator to choose to love yourself purely.

From the beginning of this earth, water has been at the start of all life. Waters were gathered into seas, lakes, rivers, and streams. [3] A mother's amniotic waters are gathered to what is called a gestation sack to prepare for life. In plants, a seed cannot begin to grow until waters are gathered unto one place: the place where the seed and soil await for beginning!

Water is an essential ingredient, but it works best when we have the right amount and when it is in the right places. Too much water or too little can create equally troublesome problems in every situation. They're just different issues. We're not just talking about drinking water. There are countless ways we use water and just as many benefits. Water can even have many patterns and so we must watch and pay attention to the lessons it can teach us.

Like the cycle of life, *birth* is the beginning doorway and *death* is the exit of mortality. There are often additional doorways we pass through between these two. If observed more closely, you begin to notice the subtleties of smaller cycles spaced at varying lengths within the cycle. There are even smaller and larger cycles within those waves as well. You might see experience cycles, life event cycles, and learning and growth cycles. Other cycles may be less easily observable: lessons learned, disciplines conquered, and weaknesses overcome.

Some patterns are realized by the practice of the principle of *obedience*. I'm not talking about the kind of obedience where you just give up your power to the point where you do whatever anyone who is over you tells you to do because they say so. That would not be wise. I'm talking about the *law* of obedience. For example, if you obey the law of studying, you can learn something. On one hand you have an action and, at the end, a consequence or a result, good or bad. In this case, if you study something good, you will have a good result.

Most people know the story of Moses. Universal Pictures+ even made a cartoon movie about it. Hollywood made one, too, starring Charlton Heston.** Television stations play the Hollywood version at least once a year during the Passover/Easter season. If you haven't seen it or aren't familiar with it, I highly recommend watching it. The story is quite inspirational, historically documented, and amazing! Once you've watched it, then come back and finish reading so you can really understand the references because it's a lot of information.

Moses and Aaron, his brother and spokesman, were in Egypt and had told Pharaoh to let his people go. (*His*, referring to Moses's God's people – the people of the one true God.) In other words, he meant the people of Israel. Pharaoh hardened his heart and said, "No!" God told Moses to go down to the water's edge the next morning where he knew Pharaoh would normally go. He was to bring the stick God had turned into a serpent with him.

Then Moses was to make another request to let the people go – and tell Pharaoh that the message was from God, so he would know the message was from him. Or else he, Moses, would lift up the rod and smite the waters in the river and it would be turned to blood, knowing that when he did this, the fish would die and the rivers would stink so badly that they would all loathe drinking the water.

Not only did God command Moses to smite the river, he also told him to smite the streams, ponds, all the pools of water in vessels of stone and wood throughout all the land of Egypt. [4] They didn't miss a single puddle of water. Every bit of it was covered by this action and warning. So Moses and Aaron did this. Not only did Pharaoh witness this event, so did all his servants!

When Pharaoh's magicians got together and duplicated something similar, Pharaoh didn't even pay any attention to them. He went home. He didn't care. There was no clean, drinkable water to be found anywhere in Egypt a whole week later, in spite of the Egyptians digging holes around the river trying to find some. They must have been getting a bit desperate after a week of not having water.

How many things do you use water for in a week? Do you drink it, cook with it, bathe in it, and water your garden or your yard? Did they have yards? Then there's laundry, cleaning house, washing hands and feet. That does not paint a pretty picture to me. There must have been a quite the groaning starting up in the land by everyone over it. Our bodies are similar in that; if a body is deprived of the things it needs, it will begin to murmur against you to try to get your attention. It will try to get help for itself. The cry can become louder and louder.

We can listen to it or go home and ignore it like it doesn't exist, like Pharaoh did. The problem doesn't go away, however. It just continues to progress and grow louder. The earlier we obey truth and balance, the sooner the body can correct things and be productive again. If we don't do what's needed and we don't obey, and truth continues being ignored, as Pharaoh learned, it can lead to great harm and possibly death.

The Pharaoh kept ignoring the truth being told to him because he didn't want to believe. It didn't agree with what he wanted to believe about his way of life or the way he was ruling in the land. He had absolutely no desire to change his ways. Even when what he loved most in his life was taken from him as a consequence of his actions, he still chose to maintain the status quo. It cost him the life of his son.

In spite of Pharaoh's wrath, Moses and God's people left Egypt and headed for the desert. All they initially wanted was to worship God on their holy days. They even would have stayed working as slaves if they'd been granted that one request.

Pharaoh could have kept all his slaves and life wouldn't have changed a whole lot for any of them. Instead, he lost them *and* his son along with all the firstborn males in his kingdom. They lost a lot more than that too. People of all ages were affected by his choice not to follow a higher law than his own.

When a law that is based on truth is obeyed, there can and will be success and not only one person will be blessed by the outcome but all those within that person's influence are also blessed. We saw in Pharaoh's land the opposite outcome demonstrated very well.

Some patterns are realized through time and life experiences that we gather along the way. Some of the obvious patterns are childhood, adulthood, and the elderly expression of our lives. In some ways we go through them once and in others, many times and in varying levels. We seek advancement. We yearn for the flowing forward momentum to ease us through each one. But coming around a gentle bend to discover raging waters or steep waterfalls can be upsetting at best and paralyzing at worst.

Moses had taken the people of Israel three days away from the Red Sea. Pharaoh's horsemen and chariots had all been drowned in their attempt to come after and recapture them after begging the people of Israel to leave. The Israelites were out in the wilderness of Shur and there was no water anywhere. [5] None. They'd just walked about thirty-one miles into the wilderness. ***

It was springtime, so it was starting to get hot during the day and cold at night. People carried babies and kids, and they were all tired and thirsty. When they went a little farther and got to the waters of Marah (literally translates to mean *bitter*) they found out it was undrinkable because the water actually *was* bitter. Scientists today believe the water at that particular spot was brackish.

We witness the children of Israel in the beginning stages of their childhood as they learned about God's ways and for his plans for them. They were wet behind the ears. They had no experience in these types of things. They were helpless and vulnerable. Without the lifesaving water that they needed, they were weak and could even very soon die!

Without water, you get kind of crabby and gripey. Your brain doesn't work well, you can't think straight, and your body temperature increases with dehydration. Along with the increase in heat your emotional temper is quicker to flare up. You quickly start arguing and bickering with people you normally wouldn't, over things that aren't worth really fighting over. Tasks that were once easy become less coordinated, and when you get dehydrated, you get clumsier. This is documented. You start to drop things more, the words start to come out wrong, and you stumble over the smallest things, like pebbles and cracks. The tiredness kicks in as your body begins to die from lack of fluids, and your blood thickens.

Without intervention by God, who inspired Moses to throw a particular type of tree in the waters of Marah, which turned the waters sweet, they might surely have died there. It would have been a fruitless break for freedom. Instead, they were obedient in their life experiences, discovered a few new things, and learned to trust just a little bit.

As Israel went along wandering for the next forty years, due to their own lack of faith and trust in God's laws, they had more experiences: wanting for bread -- to have manna provided for them, then ungrateful and misguidedly wanting meat when God was trying to purify them -- quail was provided. These were all tests and trials to see if they would learn to be obedient to these certain basic laws.

Water has laws. How your body governs water also has laws. If you break the laws, you hurt your body. Your body cannot then, in turn, help you in your goals, in accomplishing vital daily functions that you don't even have to think about. Most of all, if you follow the laws of water, you can feel and look better too! It's the simplest and most cost effective beauty treatment not marketed as such, and it's readily available. It's one of the most affordable and highly effective preventative nutrients you can take into your body.

Are you going to be perfect at testing out and mastering a new law the first time? If you are like the rest of us, most likely you will not be. Very possibly it will take a lot of trial and error. Perhaps even some retesting, like the Israelites had to go through. It may take repeatedly starting again.

There will need to be practice and perseverance on your part, but you can reach your goals. It took me a lot of trial and error with a lot of different methods before I figured out really good ways of hydrating. There are additional things needed to help hold and absorb that water, too, which I'll go into a little bit more in the next book. Needless to say, there are internal and external things you can start doing today that will be very helpful tomorrow.

Even with the best laid plans, sometimes things don't go the way we intend. We can beat ourselves up over it, using our internal trauma voice, or we can make a different choice. We can use our self-love voice that tells us, yes, I did or didn't do x, y, z... and I now have this consequence, but it's okay. I'm okay.

I can still love me because I'm learning. There is no "perfect" unflawed way for me to get through this but the way I'm going. And it's perfectly all right! I love myself enough to give it another try and another until I've mastered it and am complete in this area and can move on to the next thing!

How can it be possible to talk to ourselves this way if we've seen the opposite all around us all our lives? It may feel absolutely impossible! It may feel wrong, backwards, and awkward. And it should. If this is not your normal response to everything you do wrong, then when you do the opposite, you are going directly against your brain's natural direction and electrical current. The brain is naturally wired to resist change in order to protect it and you. We know this from neuroscience. We've also learned that the brain can be reprogrammed, much like a computer. We can create new habits and patterns in our lives and our activities by changing what we do and the way we think.

We get stuck in these ruts we're used to running in everything from our thoughts to our words, even our behaviors. Trials and adversities become part of these cycles right from the start as part of the common lot of man. We can be permanently affected by them, – damaged, changed, and hurt forever. We can even amplify their effects upon us, increasing the damage done to the priceless beings we truly are.

We can even convince ourselves that these amplifications are appropriate, that we *deserve* them, or that they must remain in place until x, y. or z changes. Until so-and-so rectifies us back to our priceless and original perfect or *whole* status. Even if we wait for that to happen, it may never in this life. Meanwhile we don't see that we don't deserve such violence and wrong doing at the hand of another, let alone by our own hands.

In 2 Samuel 14:14 [6] of the Old Testament, we find an exquisite example of this where a so-called wise woman went to Kind David speaking of water spilt upon the ground, which cannot be gathered up again; yet God doth devise means that his banished be not expelled from him.

Now, as regular people, we would spill water on the ground and not be able to get it back. It would absorb into the earth and be gone. Things are not always what they appear to be in the moment, or even any of the time. With experience we can look back and see how sometimes things we thought and things we did were a certain way. After going further down a road, though, we see more where we might have thought wrongly, believed incorrectly, and chosen mistakenly.

To understand this principle more fully we need to understand what was going on in 2 Samuel that led up to the wise woman coming before the king making this strange statement. To preface, this story is a bit sad and traumatic, and I apologize in advance to any who may be affected by it. It must be told, though. And I hope that even the most tender-hearted person will read it and find a merciful lesson in it.

So once upon a day gone by, there was a real King David. He had many wives and many children. The story starts with two of his sons, who were half-brothers, Amnon and Absalom. Absalom was a beautiful, flawless, perfect-looking man, probably even down to his pearly teeth. But it was Amnon who was the chosen heir to the throne.

It just so happened that Absalom had a vexingly fair sister named Tamar, and Amnon was absolutely beside himself with desire to have his way with her. His subtle cousin who also happened to be his friend (this was not Absalom, the half-brother) devised a plan for Amnon to have opportunity to be alone with her at the king's command; – David was not aware of the plot but became an unwitting participant in it. To spare those who are sensitive to this story I will spare the details of exactly how, where, and when.

Suffice to say, when Tamar refused Amnon's request to lie with him, he raped her. Now, this would be bad enough as it was. She was a princess and a virgin and wore the royal robes showing her purity and status. Anyone looking at her could easily identify her as such.

Tamar was well known as a good, virtuous woman who knew the law. She well knew this was not an appropriate activity and also inappropriate time, and especially not with a brother. This one major act alone caused enough damage against her that would have major repercussions the rest of her life. It would destroy her status, her ability to marry, etc... She knew this, and, gave Amnon every opportunity to be a different kind of man, and even suggested he request from the king that he could marry her first.

Amnon wanted nothing to do with anything she said and took her virginity against her will anyway. She understood the ramifications of what he had done to her and how wrong it was and begged him to rectify the situation as he had one more chance to be somewhat honorable. Instead, he threw her out on the streets and locked the doors behind her. This additional action that he took against her made this an even worse offense.

Tamar publicly proclaimed the wrong that was done to her by covering her head in ashes and tearing her clothing that marked her as a daughter of the king and a virgin. Her brother Absalom was angry at Amnon over her rape, and so Absalom took her into his own house and took care of her after that for the rest of his life as she no longer had the option to be married.

Her father, the king, and unwitting party to the scheme, was also very angry once he found out what happened. However, he did not do anything about it. He did nothing to punish his oldest son, Amnon, whom he loved, and was the guilty party even though it destroyed his daughter's entire life. Because King David chose not to act against him and hold him accountable to the law, Absalom's hands were tied and he could not do anything else to help his sister or help restore her.

Two years passed and nothing changed in Amnon's life other than that he now hated Tamar more than he originally lusted after her. No punishment for and no restitution by Amnon, King David, and no healing or justice for Tamar or Absalom. Absalom couldn't take it anymore and plotted to murder Amnon to avenge his sister's rape. (Or was it vengeance?)

Absalom finally invited his half-brother Amnon to a sheep shearing festival where he had his servants murder his half-brother. The rest of King David's sons, who were also invited, fled back to the palace, but before they arrived, several people told King David that *all* of his sons were murdered.

Absalom went into hiding at his grandfather's house on his mother's side, who happened to be the neighboring king. The details came out to King David that only Amnon was dead and it was done by Absalom's servants.

David could not take military action against Absalom without starting a war with Geshur, the neighboring kingdom. His top military general Joab acted to reconcile the father (David) and son (Absalom) in order to keep the nations from going to war. These actions end up *still* ended up leading to a civil war when Absalom later tried to take the throne from his father, King David.

This is the point where we find the wise woman, disguised as a widow, prostrating herself before the king. She was there under the guise of a make-believe situation that paralleled the king's dilemma with his two sons and daughter Tamar. The case she presented to him legally required him to rule between two conflicting principles in Israelite justice. One was the right of the family clan to exact justice or blood revenge. The other was the survival of the house of the father. Which would win: justice or mercy?

Once the wise woman had said all that Joab told her to say, she had the king in her trap. She then brought up Absalom's case. The woman made the case that God himself grants mercy over justice and reminded him of the story of Cain and Abel. She then asked him if God does not take the initiative of bringing the banished home.

King David realized Joab was behind everything. Once the realization was made, Joab fell on his face before the king, blessing him for hearing his request. He went back and retrieved Absalom to Jerusalem. It seems all is rectified between them now. Except we have to ask ourselves is the wise woman's wisdom really wisdom?

The two cases are not really parallel. The widow's fictional sons, acting in the spur of the moment in passion to murder; and Absalom's actions were definitely premeditated as likewise was Amnon's premeditated rape of Tamar, his half-sister.

From Absalom's perspective, his plan couldn't have gone any better. He was able to exact revenge for his sister and removed his brother from between him and the throne. The reconciliation between the king and his son, Absalom as much as the woman's wisdom really wasn't wisdom the successful reconciliation was not really successful either.

Absalom spent two years being back home but not truly being reconciled. His father refused to look at him ever again. To outside appearances, all everyone else saw was a young, handsome, and virile king-to-be in Absalom.

For our purposes here with water and our goals, we could say, "What kind of person should I be to myself and my progress? Should I be the looking-perfect-and-flawless-at-everything-all-the-time but hollow, empty, and going nowhere type or the broken-hearted, humble, self-forgiving but loving, strong, and kind type?"

One lesson is that waiting around for reconciliation does not mean there will be a restoration in this life. If we continue to dwell on it, it can destroy not only our life but the lives of those around us. Part of not sitting around waiting for reconciliation comes in the tiny little things we do every day; drinking water, resting, exercising, eating right, etc... It also includes how we think about ourselves and the things we've experienced in this mortal life.

Like water washes away and cleanses us, spiritual cleansing restores us. The story of the prodigal son also shows us no matter how low our life gets, we can turn around and go back to the God we once had. It may take struggle and time but the effort will be well worth it.

Chapter 3
Job

THE COLORS AND SHAPES of our life cycles of trial and adversity vary from you to me. The way they affect us varies as widely as their diversity. We see these in some of the examples given already. You may even recognize some easily identified behaviors develop as we go through childhood. Selfishness, greed, the loss of one's power or strength are just a few of them. Many times, the body grows up but the mind does not. It gets stuck in a traumatic childhood event and doesn't know how to get out of it.

We repeat the pattern and the trauma over and over until its recognized, identified, and restored to its forward progressing path. We then continue onward, emotionally developing, and eventually catching up to our physical growth. If we have experienced multiple traumas – and many of us have – it can take some time to work through these cycles. Luckily, water is a very good record keeper and it records everything going on it the body, mind, and emotions. Bones are incredible storage units.

Many of us are still stuck emotionally in our childhood stage. If you watch for it, you will see versions of tantrums to get what a person wants; you may see bullying and a lot of other things. Quietly watch people interact. Your observations are just for you and your learning process. As you are learning, you may not always be right in your observations, so be very careful not to put your perceptions of what you see onto anyone else. Do not make them a topic of conversation or gossip with others people often mishear and, misunderstand, and you could really hurt a person's reputation if you are wrong.

You can then apply identifying these things within yourself. As you watch and apply to your life situation, you may uncover the secrets to your aversion to drinking more water, bathing, eating right, exercising or whatever self-care need you happen to be neglecting at present. Failing to take responsibility for not doing these basic loving things for yourself falls under this umbrella too.

When I was a child, I thought as I child and acted as a child. We can choose to stay as children in our traumas and keep doing things as we've always done. The body wants to heal itself and will give us lots of opportunities to do so to move us towards the things we truly desire.

Are we waiting for an invitation to start healing these traumas before we can even begin to recover? Do we not know where the first step is in order to discover what the traumas are and how to begin healing them? Are we waiting on God's vengeance to be enacted upon our abusers? What is it that seems to be holding things up, and what do we need in order to have the strength and courage to move forward?

In waiting for God's retribution, do we become our own jailers? Do we promise to release ourselves on a day that never comes in our lifetimes because we cannot allow ourselves to ever let go of what happened to us until we actually see the punishment meted out to the abusers? Have we been trained culturally or socially to glorify the watching of punishment dished out and reveling in it? Have we been trained to enjoy or possibly to even seek out watching or even participating in the cruelty and harm of another person?

My heart bore a sorrow hidden so deep that memory could not even find it. For far too long, it has cloaked a burden so heavy that it lay waiting, festering for a chance to become unburied and heard. It struggled for every chance to send up signals that it was there waiting to come into the light of day.

Many people carry such burdens. They remain deep in the subconscious until it is safe enough to face them. These things wait silently until there is enough emotional and physical strength to look these burdens square in the face. It can be a day that people are filled with dread about having to deal with and will do everything to avoid, or it can be a day people can look forward to with some semblance of gratitude for the liberation it gives them that they long for. That day may begin in darkness, mourning, and awfulness, but it can turn into a perfect brightness of hope, purity, and surety.

After the Son of God began showing forth miracles at the earliest start of his ministry, he called his twelve apostles. He took them with him and stood in the plain along with a very large group of people. They gathered from all around to hear him speak and be healed by him. And he did just that. He healed those with unclean and evil spirits. And so impressed and empowered were the people by these healings that they *all* sought to touch him and be healed. There was healing power that went out of him and healed all who were present.

Then he looked upon his disciples, those who believed in and followed his teachings. He told them a few of the blessings that were theirs to claim. The poor's kingdom could be the kingdom of God. Those who hungered could be filled. And he told them that those who now wept could have the power and strength given to them to laugh.

It is there within us already. We only need call upon it and ask to access it and then live the correct principles that make it possible.

I know what you're thinking. How do we call upon this power within us also known as the power of prayer? When we pray our hearts need to be drawn to our Savior. We need to try to first align *our will* to his. And if we are gathered with at least two or three others also agreeing with his will and your request, he has promised to be there with us. The power of the prayer is increased exponentially. You must cast out *all* your doubt and have faith that what you ask will be given. We are much more powerful than we realize. We must forgive others who hurt us if we want to be forgiven.

In Luke 11:1-13 God taught his disciples to pray after he had been praying by himself and so he told them a formal pattern to follow.

- Compliment, thank, and praise God
- Ask for those things needed to survive
- Ask for forgiveness for their wrongs to others as they forgive those in debt to them
- Ask not to be led to temptations
- End the prayer in Jesus' name, our advocate

Following this order is not always necessary and sometimes not conducive to the situation. I give you a very personal and painful example from my own life. I am constantly trying to improve myself and to let go of the many pains and offenses that have been done to me. From time to time my brain knows when I can deal with letting go of something else. And so, as my body knew and signaled something big was coming forth while I was trying to write this very chapter, my mind consciously could not register it for weeks and going into months. Frustration grew as the brain struggled, resisting any changes to the familiar status quo. Systems and functions shut down in favor of diverting energy towards this singular task to suppress and subdue what my present awareness viewed as a mortal enemy.

As the point arrived when the brain began losing the battle, the details and pieces arose like a massive puzzle tossed recklessly on the floor. And then the pieces began to move and rearrange themselves in my mind until they finally came to rest in one complete, horrifying picture. Things awful enough, my conscious wanted to deny them, the most damaging betrayal of all confirmed as reality.

Realizations, the stuffed emotions of the past that could not be dealt with, then flooded out, destroying everything in their path. The aftermath, I knew, would be brutal and take a long time to clean up. Life all ragged, broken, and weak just struggling to stand would be in my near future. The heart and blood cried for justice to be satisfied. Time had run out for the accused and so justice could not be in this life for me. The villain will know and experience every bit of my grief and pain when they go through God's sentencing on judgment day.

Knowing this, I feel great pity and hope that God will also be merciful to this guilty party. The law and mercy stand ruling together, hand in hand. Struggling under this new *old* burden of knowledge and in the moment preferring death to feeling the pain, betrayal, and understanding, a gift is sent in the form of the kind words of strangers and loved ones. It was the balm I needed, while blinded by the acute new pains.

Then it came; the hope for healing if I could take the first step toward asking for help. "Please, take this from me. Take all of it, if it's in my best interests, and for my ultimate healing and benefit! I've already been working on forgiving other aspects, so please, I give full permission to take it all" my soul cried. And I meant it on every level.

Over the next few hours, anguish dissipated until it was gone. Do things always pass so quickly? No. But sometimes they can and do. There are a variety of reasons why it can take longer sometimes. It can be affected by the amount of other damage or trauma in front of it needing release or repair first, the amount of nutritional support the body has available for it at that time in relation to all your other experiences, traumas, or life at that particular moment. Layers...It can also have to do with your ability to act on your healing and helping the body to let go too. There may also be varying coping skills, the amount of support you feel you have, and a myriad of other things too.

Sometimes a wave of emotion comes up to be released so unexpectedly that it knocks you off your feet. It can be so overwhelming that all your spirit can do is cry out "Oh, God!" There can be no plea more desperate for relief. No cry of anguish is more painful.

The weight and pressure of agonizing traumas working their way out of the body, at times too great to be borne alone, seeks deliverance for the one who cannot help themselves remove the brokenness. Its death grip seems to have a relentless hold, and then it releases, having forever lost its grip upon you.

Then as great as the horror, in floods an equally exquisite and, complete joy, and lightness. Yet in the darkest moment, you cannot foresee or even hope such an outcome is possible. Alone, trying to do it by yourself, it is not. Yet with help, it can be and is.

The ego would have you think and believe that you have to do it on your own in life. It would have you convinced that there is no one you can rely upon except *yourself*. Or that you must give up all your agency and emotional, physical, and spiritual power to another *authority*. For some, this may be a government. For others, it may be a medical professional. It might even be to another person: a parent, spouse, a friend, or a sibling.

Each of these things may be helpful, when used only for their intended purpose. The other person to whom you gave your power may not even be aware you did so or be guilty of using your power against you or for a single evil purpose. It is something that may or may not be true, but it is worth considering.

Each of these relationships on their own may be helpful when used only for their intended purpose in the proper way. Not used in the right way, they become chains around our necks when we give others *our* power that does not belong to them. At times we unknowingly place the chains around our own necks, thinking it is being placed around someone else's and then proceed to choke our emotional selves while trying to hurt other people. No one else can know what's best for you. Only your creator can know that. All these other groups and people should only be viewed in the capacity for which they were intended and not as crutches.

A government's main job – and only job, really – is to protect the borders of the country from war. A government *has* no other job: they are not policemen, babysitters, educators, tax makers, guardians, or parents to take care of you. Our government is also not a health care provider or a ruler. *We* are these people individually. Until you can take your own power back and maintain your responsibility for each of these things, you will not be able to truly understand nor fulfill your relationship to hydration. One thing touches every other thing in life, and they are all inseparable. True dualities cannot continue to exist in the same time and space. In the end, one or the other will win out. You will love the one or the other, or you will cling to the one and despise the other. They cannot exist equally together. It is the same in the body.

The role of a medical professional is important. They diagnose what they can find to the best of their ability. Just as in governments, people are not all well suited to their tasks. It's important that you choose carefully whom you work with and then still proceed with caution. There are imposters in every industry. Make sure you address the spiritual aspects of your condition before *and* after a medical appointment. Have you worked on the emotional aspects related to it too? Physical, emotional, and spiritual hydration alone can improve and prevent a lot of health issues.

The next order of business is to treat with mild herbs and mild foods in pre-early stages. This includes but is not limited to things like certain herbal plants, bone broth, steamed fruits and vegetables (raw and cooked). We'll go into this more in detail in the next book concerning the importance of foods. For now, think wholesome, natural foods, water, homemade soups, and cooked vegetables.

When considering how to cook foods, I mean cooked on the stove and not in a microwave. These foods need to be heated at lower temperatures to maintain as much of the nutrient content as possible. Once you've exhausted these avenues without success, the next course of action should be medicine.

That is not to say if you already have a full-blown medical condition that *already* requires a doctor's help that you should not proceed to go directly to see one. Use these things together. Merely, it draws attention to a lot of symptoms like heart palpitations, tiredness, tingling and numbness, etc. that are *not* indicators of a physical problem yet but can be symptoms of a spiritual or emotional imbalance which can be easily and quickly corrected. Consider the possibility.

The body uses the most effective tools to get your attention to remedy a situation before it actually becomes a true physical problem. It is the loud last cry for help before it's too late. These can be easily treated yourself or with a little help from a nutritionist or other natural modalities.

Parents are important in their role throughout our lives. None are perfect, to be sure. We are all only human, trying to do the best we can with the experiences we've had and the past that we were given as well as our interpretation of it to pass on to the next generation. Parents can sometimes be good examples and lessons in what *not* to do. As children, we rely completely on parents or guardians for our very lives. Our food, shelter, love and protection all come through them. At least, they should. There's not a lot of agency available to a child unless we allow them opportunities to try it out.

As we grow up and get older, the number of choices associated with agency should change. We begin to develop a sense of our own selves and where we fit in the world. We learn about agency, responsibility, and self. We learn about liberties. We begin to become equals. And eventually in life our roles change. Then *we* become the provider, protector, and caretaker.

This natural transition through life is necessary. If one side dominates for too long or too much, it creates death for both parties. This can occur whether it is realized or not. Both sides must come to understand the differences and different needs of the other person for things to flow as they should. Our differences are what bless and help each other. It may be difficult to appreciate them when they are not exactly the same as ours but if we can step out of egos long enough to see reality its true form, we will find the benefits.

It can be just as easy to hand over our power to a spouse, friend, or sibling as it can be to a parent. The habit of wanting to not take responsibility for ourselves can invade every part of life. Not only do we not grow in these situations, we actually go backwards in our progress. When this happens, we become stagnant, just like a swamp. Stagnation is a breeding ground for all types of disease and illness. Clean it out, take your power back, and keep your life flowing in a healthy, calm, happy way. The goal is balance and harmony of both the masculine and feminine in all aspects of life.

As convenient as it may seem to stay in the state of ego or giving up our power, it prevents blessings. It stops us from receiving the gifts of feeling loved, accepted, appreciated, and more. It blocks from view the supportive loved ones who want to help. It prevents us from letting go and forgiving ourselves and others. That's exhausting, and it uses up a lot of valuable resources that could be much better spent in other areas. If there is less pain, sickness, and exhaustion what could there be more of instead? No really. Stop and take a moment to think about that...what could there be? And it starts with the various aspects of water.

We can experience many different types of things in life and it is our choice a lot more than we think how we view what happens to us. Do we unintentionally throw ourselves into a prison with only barely enough moldy bread and bad water to keep ourselves alive until the wrongs against us are rectified, like King Ahab did to the prophet Micaiah? [7] He didn't deserve that sort of treatment. We don't either.

In case you're unfamiliar with this bit of history, we have to go way back in time to about 853 B.C. There had been a two-year war with Syria followed by three years of no war. Assyrian records described the major battle fought at Qarqar on the Orontes River at that time. Though Assyria claimed victory, later events showed they were stopped from further advancement southward. Since King Ahab had neutralized the Assyrian threat, he turned his attention to the unfinished conflict with Syria.

The peaceful time started immediately after the second war with Ben-hadad. During this period, a coalition or alliance was formed between Ben-hadad, Ahab, and ten other kings to repel an Assyrian invasion. King Jehoshaphat was a good king, who was, legally related to King Ahab through the marriage of his son Jehoram to Ahab and Jezebel's daughter Athaliah. So Ahab's disputes became the family affairs of all Israel.

Up to that point, relationships had not been so good between the two nations due to the breaking up of the twelve tribes into Judah and Israel. Since Jehoram and Athalia's marriage, at least King Ahab and King Jehoshaphat were in touch, and Syria was a common enemy. When Ben-hadad recaptured Ramoth in Gilead, which was a Levitical city east of the Jordan River, on the north border of Gad (the home of Jephtha, he did not return possession of it to Israel as he had promised. (It was also a key administrative center in Solomon's kingdom.)

We can see all kinds of problems cropping up resulting from broken promises, people's choices, and impatience. Ahab didn't feel confident that his troops could take the land back from Ben-hadad on their own and not only did he want Judah's troops to help him, he also wanted Judah's God to help him.

When Ahab asked Jehoshaphat for help, Jehoshaphat could have said no but their kids were now married, and he probably also didn't like the idea of Syria holding a town so close to his territory, so he quickly told Ahab in no simpler terms than what's mine is yours. He followed this up, however, with the reminder to ask the will of God first before going into battle, as had been done in the past. (See 1 Samuel 9:13, 23:1-5, 2 Samuel 2:1; 5:19-25; and 2 Kings 3:11-20.)

Ahab gathered up four hundred prophets of Asherah who all gave him the green light to go to battle against Syria. Jehoshaphat wanted a true prophet of the Lord to tell them if they should go up or not. It was known these four hundred prophets of Asherah were the type of people who would tell the king whatever flattering words he wanted to hear, not necessarily what was true. Ahab finally admitted that there was only one true prophet, Micaiah, but said that he didn't like him. He told Jehoshaphat that it was because he never had anything nice to say (about him, the king) and he only told the truth.

Someone was sent to fetch Micaiah from prison. Probably, because Ahab didn't like his last prophecy that went against him, he knew exactly where Micaiah was. Ahab was so desperate for Jehoshaphat's help he seemed willing to risk another bad report from the true prophet. The officer suggested Micaiah say the same thing the other so-called prophets were saying, that way the king would be happy. Micaiah would not be swayed and told the officer that he would only say what God told him to say.

They arrived to find both kings all dressed up along with the false prophets and the court. The prophets were presenting King Ahab with all sorts of things like virtually unbreakable horns of iron, a symbol of power, while telling him to go up to Ramoth-Gilead and prosper.

Each false prophet repeated the pattern, promising victory in attacking Syria and taking

Ramoth-Gilead. After seeing all of this happening, the messenger sent to collect Micaiah, urged him strongly what to say. Micaiah swore he would only speak the words the Lord gave him to speak. He then sarcastically told the king to go up to battle and that the Lord would prosper him.

Ahab, being an astute man, detected the sarcasm and demanded that Micaiah tell him what he really believed, in the name of the Lord. Micaiah made sure that the king actually wanted to know what the Lord's will was because he didn't ask for that the first time. That's why Micaiah gave him a ridiculous answer! King Ahab demanded that he wanted the absolute truth from the Lord.

Micaiah then revealed what God showed to him would happen if King Ahab went up to battle against Syria. That was, that the king would die and his army would be scattered. Of course, Ahab turned to Jehoshaphat and said, "See, didn't I tell you he would prophesy no good about me, but only evil?" He meant to sway Jehoshaphat to the idea that the prophet only said that to spite him and intended him only malice, so it couldn't be from God, and they should just disregard *everything* he said. Three years before, Micaiah had told him he would die for letting Ben-hadad go, but so far it hadn't proven true, and so neither would this.

Jehoshaphat was an easy-going man and too easily believing as well. He believed Ahab and chose to go to war with him. Still, Ahab knew he had displeased God more than once. He already knew he shouldn't expect any other outcomes from God's revelations. Because Ahab presented what Micaiah told him about God's will in such a bad light, he stressed to him even more, so he would not be able to mistake that what he said was coming from God and not from him out of malice.

Micaiah said he saw God sitting on his throne, which was a pattern of Ahab and Jehoshaphat sitting on their thrones. He saw the hosts of heaven on his right and left hand waiting to do his will. An evil spirit came forth and said he would persuade Ahab to go up to battle. He sent spirits to speak through the four hundred false prophets who all said for Ahab to go up to battle. But unbeknownst to him, by going up to battle, he would actually end up bringing about his own ruin, which had been appointed unto him. This also fulfilled the prophecy of Micaiah against Ahab from three years before.

There were a few choice insults exchanged between Zedekiah, the head speaker for the false prophets accompanied by a disgusted slap to Micaiah's face for his unpleasant prophecy. This led Micaiah to tell Zedekiah that he would find out himself just how accurate his prophecy was when he hid himself in an inner chamber.

The King of Israel told his officers to take Micaiah back to jail where he was to be held until his own peaceful return and for Micaiah to be barely kept alive. He undoubtedly planned to have the prophet killed when he came back. The prophets last days were to be cruelly miserable and of the most meager means allowed. Micaiah said to the king, "*If* you return," and indeed, the king did not.

Ahab would hold the truth prisoner and then murder it. The truth did not fit in the box he wanted, and so he tossed it out. However, he did not toss it out with the intent to let it be free. He threw it into a locked box. He denied it light, nourishment, good, clean water, and love. More than merely murder an innocent man under the guise of hypocrisy, he wanted to take away the very hope of the prophet by depriving him of almost everything that could sustain his very life. Are we guilty of the same against someone in our own lives, against our own lives?

Is it more excusable to emotionally murder someone or, furthermore, ourselves than it is to physically commit murder against a person or even a beast? If you believe in a supreme creator the answer has to be an emphatic no! It cannot be reasoned either that you aren't hurting anyone else if you are only hurting yourself. What you do, think, and say to yourself becomes part of your DNA and also affects your vibrational frequency or personal current. That frequency extends out from your physical body. Every person you come into contact with is affected by the energy wavelength of your thoughts, words, and actions. You can leave a positive or negative trace in their field. Even your missing interactions affect those around you.

No matter how much you try to stop life from happening by the choices you make and don't make, you cannot stop the river of life from flowing. This river intends to flow freely on its course. You may think you can dam up the river and block its flow forever, but you'll only end up with a mucky brackish pond. It will become a deeper lake as you scramble to build higher and wider walls. As it becomes stagnant, it will start to stink. No matter how fast you build or how wide, one day that dam is going to break. It will be bigger and harder to deal with the longer you wait.

Our lives are much like nature. We may experience smaller scale versions with our bodies like earthquakes, avalanches, and mudslides when things affect us or are shifting whether making way for better or worse things. I will leave it up to your imagination how these events might manifest in the various forms within the body.

Think about how the waters wear down the stones and wash away the things which grow out of the dust of the earth and destroy the hope of man.

[8] We too can be worn down, worn away until our hope is completely destroyed, if we are not careful. We can prevent this from happening by consciously acting to prevent such things by doing things as properly hydrating and also participating in all twelve resources we talked about in the book *"Member Heal Thyself."*

A perfect, flawless life without any trials is what we hope for but that is not realistic. We could not grow, learn, or experience opposition without trials and opposition. We can view the fact that we have these differences and challenges as a sign of great trust by a loving Father in our abilities to have experiences, to survive, and to learn to find solutions that work better. Some will have a greater chance at this from slower growth and others faster due to each of our own varying degrees of natural gifts, talents, and skills. Neither is better, they just offer different things that the others cannot.

Like water wearing away the stones, we can let ourselves be worn away until there is nothing left simply by doing nothing at all. We can choose to be acted upon by others, or we can choose to act and choose the results and consequences we want to experience in this life. This option is to refill ourselves from the fountain of the water of life and practice the rest of the twelve resources.

Our hopes can be completely destroyed by the overwhelming waters of trapped emotions, poor health habits, and/or poor spiritual choices. Any imbalance in our wholeness equates to an imbalance of all things. The fountain of the water of life can wash away all the rough places and, the undesirable, broken parts. It can leave us with a completeness we've never before known.

Some of us who have a lot of trials may feel like we have a touch of Job in our lives. Not the blessed, rich Job; the Job who was tested and, stripped of all possessions and family life. Systematically losing every good thing in every area can take a toll on a person, break their spirit, and make them weep.

Job was a righteous, hardworking man who had accumulated great wealth, many servants, and had a very large family. He lost his oxen and servants who were out plowing in a field to the Sabeans while his children were having dinner at the oldest brother's house. All his servants there were killed but one, and the animals were stolen.

While this remaining servant was telling him what happened, another servant arrived to tell him that the fire of God fell from the heaven (maybe lightning or a meteor?) and burned up all his sheep and the servants who were there except for him.

While the second guy was telling Job what had happened, a third servant arrived, also bearing bad news. Three bands of Chaldeans stole all his camels and killed all the servants that were with him but him. He alone escaped to come and tell him.

Yet *another* servant arrived to tell him a huge wind came from the wilderness and destroyed the house where all his children were gathered, killing everyone but him.

Job could have cursed God, punished himself for deserving such disasters, or curled up and died just from the grief, but he didn't. He lifted himself up, mourned his many losses that day (and probably many days after), and chose to worship. He acknowledged that he came into the world with nothing and that he would also leave this life with nothing. He didn't blame it on God. He understood the universal law to which all men are accountable, and he was no exception.

Later, Job became infected head to toe with boils. His wife asked him how he could keep his integrity like that and told him to curse God and die. She must have thought by this point he might be better off dead than having all this happen to him. He told his wife that she was talking like the foolish women in town. He understood there was and is opposition in life. There was and is good and bad. There was and is balance in all things.

Job's friends heard of his trouble and came to comfort him and mourn with him. Before they even got close, they realized that they didn't even recognize him. They wept, tore their mantles (long, sleeveless cloaks) and sprinkled dust on their heads towards heaven as a sign of their grief and mourning. They sat with him for seven days and nights not speaking a single word to him. Job's grief was so very great, and they could feel it.

After the seven days and nights had passed, Job said he wished he'd never been born or that he had died at birth. His grief and pain had reached a point he could no longer bear. His greatest fears had become his reality. His friends tried to counsel and advise him, but Job became angry and lashed out at them because all he wanted was pity and felt betrayed by those who should have understood him. They all had a very deep conversation back and forth about Job's plight and about God.

God chastised Job, and Job was humbled and repented of his lack of understanding of God's power and wisdom. God also chastised Job's three friends for not speaking rightly of Job and told them to repent and how, so that they would be accepted by him. Then, Job's trials were turned around, and he ended up being blessed with more of everything that he'd had before, many times over.

Much like Job, when we are in the middle of our deepest afflictions and sorrows, we might see no end in sight. We may see no purpose for our suffering. Perhaps, we will feel all hope is lost, forever. We might even feel that the waters have worn down *our* stones and removed every bit of life *we* have left. The hope we had left might seem so far destroyed, that it can never come back again. But we can learn from Job's story, and mine, and that of others, that our pain is just a hallway. And hallways are just temporary places of transition from one place to another or from one state of being to another.

Hydration is a hallway of sorts. It allows transitions to occur. Whether the hydration is associated with physical water, emotional, or spiritual, they can all create a transition. In the river of our lives, these trials can change our course, bury us, or block our true flowing direction – or at least temporarily block us. Some physical water allows our blood to move our nutrients, our air, the waste products, and more from one place to another. Things go in and others come out.

In the same way, spiritual hydration helps the same processes in a different way. It can help by bringing in some good and nourishing strength and light for our spirits. This hydration helps with the removal of the old waste ideas, false perceptions and traditions, and untruths we've erroneously believed. The cleaner that water is and the purer the source of it is, the more we are able to receive from it.

In the right balance, water allows everything to move at their proper paces. Things can work the way they're supposed to. We can eliminate the things we don't want in our thoughts, from our behaviors, and from our lives a lot more easily. How quickly this process can happen depends on our processing speed, so be patient with yourself and with others.

Some people will be able to process more quickly but usually are only working through more superficial layers. If this is you, beware of feeling better *enough* without still having some things to clear out still. Be careful that you don't get to a prior level of health when you didn't feel as bad as you may now. Feeling comfortable *enough* can be a deceptive trap in itself, leaving you feeling you are whole again and your work is done. All you've done is just remove the most painful layer on top, but the rest of the pain, the root, and the source that created that so-called pain plant continues to grow within you, and is still there, and will grow back.

These are the sad tales you hear about with major medical health traumas; people who tried alternative medicine or a holistic approach to healing themselves, who saw results, and then turned around and died after all the work they did.

In their own opinion they thought they were healed *enough*.

A few months or years later they end up getting sick again. This is usually because they didn't finish and continue the work until they got the whole thing worked out. They quit living in their new habits and went back to all the things they did before. Thought patterns, old ways of eating and drinking or not drinking, and old lifestyles slowly crept back in because old habits die hard and causes the old problems to return and grow back very quickly and usually much more aggressively. This is medically documented substantially.

Once you start feeding the root source of pain and fertilizing it with all the old habits again, it's just going to consider that you gave it a good hard pruning but now you've given it the signal to grow back *bigger, faster* and *stronger*. Plus now you've not had time to rebuild your wellness warehouse to fight back with so, you have no ammunition left to go to war. It's so important to trust your body about your progress, the professionals who are trying to help you who are much more familiar with these things and how they work, and beware the other "voices" within you. Even more important is to stay in touch with the Big Guy upstairs.

Watch out for the voice of your own ego. It can really trip you up, making you think or feel maybe that your higher power is telling you that *you* know what's best for you or which way to go. The ego likes to make us think *it* is our higher power. The ego comes a lot from a place of pride. Not the good kind of pride as in the pride of a job well done. That's more like being well-pleased.

The pride I refer to is the one that causes you to set your jaw and hardness comes to your heart. It's a kind of stubbornness that comes along when you know you should do something good, right, or correct, but just to be contrary you don't. It's a form of self-sabotage. Sometimes we are consciously aware of it, and sometimes it's a sub-conscious reaction, especially when it's associated with a trauma trigger response. Either way the results are the same. We remove ourselves from balance, power, and wellness.

I grew up eating pretty healthy, but I also ate things everyone else was eating like fast food occasionally, desserts, processed packaged boxed foods, etc. I lived with my family in a farming community, so we had access to lots of produce. Like you, perhaps, I heard all the comments about not being able to afford buying organic foods because they were more expensive or too expensive.

I believed them too. I grew up poor due to unplanned and unexpected life circumstances. I struggled with finances a lot of my life growing up due to not having hardly any money. I had to budget carefully and was not in a position yet with my health to start focusing on fixing certain things. It's a process, a journey, not an instant destination.

Water filters and pitchers were barely coming into my awareness and I had no idea of just how important they were going to be to have as one part of my basic necessities. There are a lot of pollutions in this world. I thought we grew up in a place with pretty safe, clean water. That's what we were *told*, at least.

After moving away to another state, I looked up some information about my own home state and discovered reports about a nuclear plant that was near where we lived. The people living in the state were blocked from seeing the information somehow but now that I was out, I could find it. I was horrified and felt betrayed.

What I learned was that the nuclear waste runoff was leaking into the groundwater supply for the long time that I had lived there and was *still* an issue. The cancer death rates in the state were extremely high but no one was told. It was kept a secret. Water treatments for the water coming into our house pipes from the treatment facility ended up not being what we were originally led to believe.

Being a sensitive person and smaller in frame, I was a lot more susceptible to the extremely high levels of all the bad things in the water. The accumulations in my own body did not help me out in the least. Sometimes, you don't realize the problems sneaking up on you in the background of habits you don't even think about from one day to the next.

Do you love a good bargain? Many of us need a bargain to meet all our basic needs just to get by in life. Despite what you may have been led to believe, you can have access to things to improve your welfare. Healthy living does not have to be just for the rich and famous! We have the promise of the great, holy God of creation he will help us. Did you know he promised to hear your cries? In Isaiah 41:17 [9] the prophet Isaiah shared the Lord's revelation for his children in just this type of situation.

"When the poor and needy seek water, and there is none, and their tongue faileth for thirst, I the Lord will hear them. I the God of Israel will not forsake them."

Remembering that water also represents the emotional and spiritual aspect in *"Member Heal Thyself"*, the concept explained is that the best way to heal ourselves is to start with the spiritual. This is not saying you have to be the religious nut-job that may or may not have beliefs that are based on false perceptions, yours or someone else's. This refers to your spirit as it pertains to your whole self.

You can get a cut on your finger and it will bleed and then start healing and, likewise, our spirits can be wounded and be in need of healing. Just as much as our bodies and minds need balance in order to thrive in life, our spirits very much need these same things.

Putting aside any preconceived notions, let us take advantage of putting things in order, just the same way as when we start eating a few more healthy foods in our diet or adding more exercise into our week. As we start doing these things, we notice we feel better and we want to do them more often. (Does this mean you're going to be praying the rosary or trying to baptize cats? No. That's not what I am talking about at all.)

Remember, we are throwing out all the preconceived notions and keep all the good true things we have learned correctly while we start rebuilding the foundation. We're not taking away anything, we are only adding to what we already have. Those old notions that we ourselves choose to toss by the wayside are based on false traditions and incorrect ideas. They can be painful to acknowledge and let go.

We might be afraid of who we are without the old false traditions and incorrect habits, or feel like letting them go invalidates past experiences. They may be painful, and we may feel we will lose everything we've worked so hard to achieve in our lives or lose who we are if we let them go. These are valid concerns. I had the same ones myself. What I learned was that I was still me, my experiences still had value maybe even more than before and everything I'd worked so hard for improved and slowly got better.

It can be unfamiliar territory, going somewhere we've never gone before. The body and brain are naturally hardwired to fear change. We resist it with everything in us. Habits are the most difficult to change over a month's time because we inevitably hit, at two or three different points, a resistance threshold. Once we break through that, it gets easier.

At different longer spaced intervals, we run across various opportunities to enter the old habit rut left over in our brain. Because that old rut is so well worn and deep, it's really easy to fall back into it again and abandon the new habit we're still developing into a nice deep rut. Just hop back onto the new track as quickly as you can and don't beat yourself up. That's all there is to it. The longer you practice your new habit, the deeper *that* rut will become, and the easier it will be to stay in it.

Emotions will come up. It's part of the process. You can't escape it, and you can only ignore it for so long. You can try to put it off. You may succeed at squashing it down for a long time.

Inevitably, emotions will come up sooner or later, and they should. We weren't meant to hold onto these things forever. Animals will shake off a traumatic experience immediately. They'll shake their body and tremble and then move on. We have been culturally conditioned to grin and bear trauma instead of releasing it and so we find our design does not work this way anymore. **** Instead we need to work it out or it becomes a serious physical problem. But now we know the steps to moving this trapped trauma when it becomes stuck.

No matter how scary it is to go through releasing our stuck emotions, it *is* possible to do it. You don't need to do it alone, and you aren't supposed to. In fact, the process works a lot easier if you have some help. There's the moral support aspect to consider. When you're down or wading through tough times, knowing you have someone in your corner on whom you can actually rely who has your back and will hold you accountable can be really motivating.

When you've exhausted all your resources and there's no one left to turn to, even if you can't afford to afford professional help (which you should show financial appreciation or some sort of exchange of appreciation for when you are receiving it), there is always one place we can turn. The help will be there even if you don't own a big house or drive a fancy car. It won't matter if you wear fine clothes or have pretty rings. You don't need to own stocks and bonds, and you don't have to be wealthy to qualify. The help will be there in the best moment, in the best timing, and in the most critical way.

Where does this help come from? You don't have to look very far. God is just a prayer away and you can invite him to be part of your journey and he'll be there for you. He has promised he will. In Isaiah God said:

"When thou passeth through the waters, I will be with thee; and through the rivers and they shall not overflow thee: when thou walkest through the fire, thou shalt not be burned; neither shall the flame kindle upon thee." [10]

God's got your back. He'll be there when you're going through the waters if you want. When you go through the rivers of sorrow, they won't overflow you. When you are walking through the fires, your sorrow and pain, you won't be burned. Not only that, but not even one little flame will light upon you. That's pretty profound. It brought tears to my eyes when I read it.

Fire in your eyes burns ever so bright when you have a clear conscience and a free soul. Where do the false perceptions come from that we cannot rely on anyone to help us let go of our emotional pain and that we can't let it go either? We can only get so far on our own, and, at some point, we have to know we cannot do it all by ourselves. Misunderstanding how God works and why he allows others the right to exercise their agency, even if it hurts someone else, can be part of the reason why we struggle with that.

We also have to remember God allows us that same right. Whether we like to admit it or not, we *too* hurt others with our words, our choices, our actions, even if we are unaware of doing so. The false concept that our lives should be and deserve to be completely free of all pain, disappointment, and harm at all times contributes to this as well. We were never promised that. In fact, we were promised we *would* experience these things as a part of the law of opposition.

There's a difference between going through darkness, pain, and suffering and holding onto it forever. Learning to let those things go, as scary as they may seem, is how we get to uncovering that fire and light so it can shine in our hearts again. Once we learn these correct principles and learn to apply and recognize them, we won't overreact when something happens and will gain great wisdom as we learn to recognize what's going on around us instead of reacting to it.

When you realize you need to go through the waters it can be painful because letting go of false ideas is hard to do. It means we have to admit to ourselves that we were wrong about something we held as an important absolute truth. Often, we have to hit rock bottom before we can be honest enough with ourselves to admit it's what we have to do so we can move onward and upward.

Where is rock bottom and how do we know when we get there? That is going to be different for every single person. There may be points along the journey you will feel like you've hit it, and then something will come along that makes you realize it was just a bump on the way down to your rock bottom.

You may try to go through the waters on your own, but you'll find that eventually you will quit, think it's not working, or change to something else mid-stream that seems better in the moment. Then it will all feel like it's not working at all. Your brain will freak you out because it doesn't want anything to change.

When you're not really ready yet, you'll go through all these sorts of things. You will think you want this new life; you may act like you want it to happen. You may even tell everyone you're ready. The full commitment doesn't come though until you and that bottom meet. And, then you realize, it's do or die time. For some of us it's literal, and for others it's figurative.

Some people are figuratively toe dippers. They're ready, and they're not. They may still be trying to decide. They'll dip their toe into the metaphorical water to see how it feels first. If it's too cold or uncomfortably warm, they'll yank their foot away in shock or surprise. Some will dip once and never return, and some will dip and re-dip.

Others will dip then slowly put in a whole foot, waiting to acclimate to the newness of the temperatures and, the sensations moving upward. They then either, dip and run or, continue to slowly enter the waters with the other foot. Next they go in up to their knees, working up the courage as they slowly enter, until they completely submerge themselves. Finally, you have those who like to dip and plunge in or completely skip the dip and jump straight in.

Which method is the best one, you might ask yourself? The answer to that is all of them. They are all movement. I know you're thinking, "not the dip and run away!" but even that is movement. Once you've dipped, even once, you can never forget that dip. Even if it was uncomfortable and an experience you don't want to repeat, you won't be able to forget that it helped things feel better even if just for a very small moment. The body will long for another dip. It can be a long time before that happens again, especially if a person hasn't hit bottom yet.

In some cases a person needs a long time to process something that is so completely opposite of their old belief system, experiences, and perceptions or even gather more resources so they can handle the changes to come. Sometimes they cannot yet comprehend what happened. That's not a bad thing. Every one of us has a different makeup than anyone else and we each have different obstacles to overcome. What might work best for you could be the worst and most damaging for me and vice versa. It might be easier for you to jump in, but I may be a better swimmer. We all have different abilities.

The first thing you need to know is that the waters are there. These are the stagnant waters of your grief, sorrow, and pain. The waters are also healing waters that can wash away the burdens you've been carrying for far too long. They can cleanse you and purify you. Nothing is too heavy or too dark. The next things after realizing these waters are there is that they are available *to* and accessible *by* you.

Isaiah shared his witness with us that healing waters are available to every single person without exception. He said "Ho," - pay attention! – "everyone that thirsts, come to the waters, and if you don't have money; come, buy, and eat; yes, come, buy wine and milk without money and without price." [11]

What he's saying here is: hey you, pay attention because I'm going to tell you something super important. You're going to want to hear this! If your injured soul is parched and dry with pain, there is a way to quench your thirst. You don't have to be rich; this is available to anyone and all you have to do is come dip yourself in this water.

Dip yourself in the healing power of grace, in the atonement. This is the very thing you need to sustain your life; your real, true life. Milk is nourishing in its truest raw form. New wine was used in sacred, holy ordinances, worship, and celebration. What God's willing to share with us is sacred and nourishing.

Maybe you've started the process of immersing yourself in the waters, or you've been thinking about it. There's the something needs to change feeling that starts pushing up. Do you push it back down, afraid you don't have the time or resources to deal with it at the moment or afraid of what people will think or say?

How many times can you squash down the desire and attempt to heal emotionally or spiritually before it all comes exploding out of you? You don't have to wait for an explosion of trauma and emotions to start dealing with it. The sooner you get going on it, the easier it will be to deal with. The vibrational frequency of the cells will change as they move up to a higher level. As you do this, others around you will feel something different. They may not know what it is, but it will affect them in a positive way. They may resist their own change, but they will feel yours. Your mere presence alone can do this as you continue to let go of the heavy, low vibrational frequencies.

When you experience this change within yourself, you'll naturally want to share it with someone else. People will ask you what changed. They'll want to know your secret to life, love, and happiness. How did you do it? You have something that they have wanted but not known where to look. A thirsty peasant on their knees in a parched, dry desert looking for the water fountain, not knowing it's water that they're looking for. All they know is that you've found something they've been searching for. You have a missing piece of their puzzle.

The closer you get to the source of that fountain, the purer the water is. It's also the sweetest there. As you start denying all the false traditions, the misconceptions, you realize this new life is just what you always wanted and it's better than what you had before. There's nothing else like it. Anything else is a cheap substitute that does not satisfy. One of the qualities of water is that it can mold its shape to whatever container it is in, and in much the same way, living water molds itself to just what we need.

There are a lot of bad traditions of using fear tactics, force, corporeal punishment, and more to convince, coerce, and cajole people towards a fountain. Over time, what the fountain is has become misconstrued, misrepresented, and even flat out falsified by both well-meaning and ill-intentioned folks. Some would have you believe the carefully disguised swamp they've led you to *is* the fountain! Mix that all up in a bowl and you get a really unpalatable side of muck! Is it any wonder so many are running for the hills to get away? In the meantime, a lot of people are simply dying of thirst.

Thirst is only one thing people are dying of. There are others too but a lot could be changed by just quenching our spirit, our soul, with the fountain of living water. We often forget how this one simple truth can make everything shift and become completely new. Just one person makes all the difference.

Take fire as an example of how a small little thing can make a big impact. One spark can light a fire. That same spark can also light up a whole forest! How does it do this? By consuming and using up all the old, dead parts of the fuel source on which it lands. What it produces is light, warmth, and heat. As it goes through its process, it becomes, greater, stronger, and more powerful. It creates more sparks and, together a mighty flame!

Fire, left unattended and not constrained by certain boundaries can be destructive and can take lives. Much in the same way, water, if left unchecked or used inappropriately, wreaks havoc in life. When used in the way it was intended, water brings life, love, and happiness. For best results use the purest water that's unadulterated, unaltered, and has no added man-made ingredients. When you start adding extra ingredients what you end up with is something like fruit punch or maybe even mud.

There was this guy. His name was Ezekiel. He had amazing dreams and he was not only a priest but he was also a prophet. One of the visions he had was of the temple of God. Previous to this he had a dream showing him the battle in the last days, of Gog and Magog, where we now live. He saw that both of them would be destroyed.

Thereafter, the holy temple of the Lord will be built. He was shown the ordinances, how it was to be built in every aspect, the roles and clothing of the priests, and more. Then the Lord brought Ezekiel back to the temple to show him something else that is very important to you and me today. It reads:

"He brought me again unto the door of the house; and behold waters issued out from under the threshold of the house eastward..." [12]

The house that Ezekiel was brought to was the temple that, the Lord had shown him in the dream. In one aspect, water is representative of the fruits of the temple. Additional promises, the covenants, and blessings are made and given there beyond the covenant we make at baptism. Baptism is the first one we make to enter in at the straight, narrow gate that leads to life eternal but it's just the entrance and not the destination. There are additional gates to go through to reach the final goal. Each gate gives us extra tools and resources we will need and ideally *want* on our journey, when we understand their importance.

The multiple covenants we make are all between us and God. He promises us certain things if we will do certain things. It's a two-sided promise, and as long as we hold up our end he is obliged to deliver on his end. He is definitely generous and we are getting the best end of the deal to be sure. He does it for us because he loves us so much.

The power of this water is infinite. As it issues out from under the threshold of the house eastward, it increases in amount and depth. It heals the land, the people, and the soul. The more we partake and are healed, the more influence the effects we experience will affect those around us. You become part of this water by the very nature of the fact that you've partaken of it.

Trials and challenges arise with any kind of positive change. Others may try to convince you that there are better things than the water or may try to ridicule you for using it and making it a core part of who you are. This happens when they see your changes and are not themselves ready to try some yet. They may want you to deny yourself the joy and hope of the water so *they* can justify staying where they are comfortable. Perhaps they just don't want you to have something they don't feel worthy or deserving of yet. No one should have that, they may say!

The apostle Peter declared to the apostles and followers of Christ:

"Can any man forbid water, that these should not be baptized, which have received the Holy Ghost as well as we?"[13]

He was referring to the uncircumcised, those not of the covenant, and those who had gathered to hear them speak. Those who had gathered there had the gift of the Holy Ghost poured out on them in that moment, and this surprised the apostles and followers.

The apostles and other followers had incorrectly assumed that only the people who were exactly like them – covenant makers and keepers already – could have this experience with the Spirit.

Sometimes we too can feel like we can't receive this outpouring in our own lives. We might feel like what's blocked must stay blocked forever. We may even feel that we deserve this blockage as a permanent fixture in our lives.

What we tend to find, both in healing spirit and the whole self with water is that water can go around, under, or eventually *through* to get to where it intends to go. Water will create something new; it will find a way. Water is part of everything. You can find the same thing with healing as well. In order to benefit from it, you must partake of it. Just as water cannot hydrate you if it is not *in* you, spiritual healing cannot mend your broken places within until you are ready to get a bit of it inside of you. We must help ourselves.

Water renews us. It refreshes and cleanses. Water represents one of the first and most important doorways we ever go through. Life begins in water, and we are born from water. When we are spiritually reborn – or baptized – again, it is in water. At times when we decide to make a U-turn in our lives, it can often be accompanied by the water of our tears.

Science has found that all kinds of hormones are released in tears when we laugh and cry. The body uses this method to cleanse itself from sadness, grief, and fear. We go from being on one side of our waters to the other. God called Joshua to take over in Moses's place so he could lead the Israelites into the land of Canaan. They'd been wandering in the desert for forty years at that point! As Joshua was speaking to the people he reminded them of their history. He said:

"Thus saith the Lord, God of Israel, your fathers dwelt on the other side of the flood in olden time, even Terah, the father of Abraham..."[14]

Healing our pain, trauma, and sorrow brings us across the floods that threaten to overwhelm us. We must come through them if we are to remove ourselves from all the dark, heavy things of our soul, whether they are mental or emotional, spiritual, or physical. We must come out! Come out of our own darkness and bring our community out with us. Share what you've learned and what you now know.

Chapter 4
Noah

Fountain of Water of Life

BEING THAT THERE IS NOW more substantial archeological evidence that has been found and verified by archeologists, we know the biblical flood actually did happen and when. (I will not be covering it; just know the information is out there for you to find.) Allow yourself first, in any case, to consider the possibility that it's true in relation to this chapter.

The verifiable data shows that the flood covered the whole earth, despite the many articles that would try to sway you to the contrary with little to no evidence. The archeological and geological proof definitively validates the story of Noah's building the ark that is recounted in the Bible. This same ark was found in the last hundred years by a humble man who has since graduated from this life. His experiences are astounding!

The remains of the ark are under close watch and being carefully guarded in the nation of Turkey and a lot of people don't know about this because it's not open for tours. This information was published in Life magazine, on the 5th of September, 1960 [+] and even covered on public television channels and shows again back in the 1980's. I watched it myself along with a lot of other people! This ark was discovered by the same man who found the chariot wheels that verified the highly likely crossing place of Moses and the people of Israel through the Red Sea when they left Egypt.
Page 128

***** The man's name who found these archeological artifacts is Ron Wyatt (1933-1999), founder of the Wyatt Museum located in Cornersville, Tennessee, where you can see some of the things he's found. His family maintains his website at: ronwyatt.com.

The discoveries that Mr. Wyatt made along with the new findings official archeologists are making today buried in the flood layers of the earth, allow us to take very seriously that the world was not in a good place before the flood. This is in spite of mighty attempts men have made to deceive and make false claims against Ron's findings to sound like facts. The Book of Revelation confirms that these last days we live in will be like unto the days of Noah. There is a lot of information now validating the flood but the most important aspect to consider for our purposes today is the physical, emotional, and spiritual ramifications of the story in relation to self-healing.

Now, because a lot of information is missing from the Bible, we do not know exactly what was going on in Noah's day or just how bad it was living then other than the few brief mentions of this and that. Things like great wickedness, giants, and the corrupted flesh of man abound; we are arriving at that level of corruption today.

We can have a lot of missing information about our situations in life, our perceptions, and

Page 129

our life stories too. We base our decisions on the little bit of information we have, trying our best to figure out what everything means and how we should move forward in the safest, least complicated way.

We may have experienced great wickedness at the hand of someone who should have protected us the most. Maybe we experienced bullying at various times in life, even as adults, by those who should have been more careful in authority positions or who decided to take advantage. It is even possible that we have been changed, hurt, or damaged by someone else's choices, which took away our agency. In a lot of ways, our lives are not that different from the days of Noah.

The days of Noah were so wicked and offensive to God – and men's hearts were filled with so much violence – that God regretted ever creating them at all. It's possible that we have witnessed things that have filled our heart with great regret and have made us lose faith in humanity as it is today.

Perhaps we have even felt a little bit of that regret over choices we have made, things we have knowingly (or even unknowingly) done against others. Some may even feel that to destroy themselves from off the face of the earth for feeling this way or that it is the only solution to rid themselves and others of the negative effects they are experiencing. But it is *not* the only solution.

The only way to undo the tormenting effects and feelings we may be experiencing is to follow the twelve resources covered in *"Member Heal Thyself"* by taking baby steps with each one. We must work through them, and then we can be free of all the anguish we may be feeling. Then we may experience the same type of cleansing that the flood gave to the earth all those thousands of years ago. We can experience a clean slate and start over.

God must be feeling great regret watching the things going on in our day now too. In Genesis, God talked to Noah. [15] He had just told him exactly how to build the ark to the last detail so that he could be prepared to save his family, the last uncorrupted flesh on the earth at that time. Sometimes God gives us inspiration of things we can do to save ourselves, as it were, from the bad traditions that we've learned that damage our health and destroy our peace.

The ark Noah was instructed to build wasn't fancy. Noah didn't have any experience building ships, but there were a lot of ships being built after the manner of man at the time. People were going all sorts of places in them, and so there was a "right way" to do these things that were established as working the best. Noah's ark didn't follow these rules.

No wonder the people all mocked him! What Noah was told to build went against what the natural man said worked. Sometimes, God asks us to do things we have no experience doing, asks us to do things in nonconventional ways, and often he teaches us as we go along something that is better.

We don't know if there wasn't time for Noah to build the ark in a different way, or if it wouldn't have functioned in some way or another except for building it the way he did. We don't know if perhaps it was told in a symbolic way so we could learn a different lesson than what we first see listening to a childhood story on our mother's knee. God always teaches in layers.

I'm sure access to different materials may have made the job a lot harder than normal if shortages were being created much like in our world today. We know the ark *was* functional. Noah and his descendants survived and multiplied across the earth. Very like Noah, we may be asked to do things in unique ways, ways that we are not accustomed to or as familiar with. But if we follow the steps, we will have a good outcome, whether sooner or later.

The next thing God told Noah was that he was bringing a flood of waters on the earth to destroy all flesh. Sometimes we get warnings too. They come in dreams, in the words from a doctor, or even a stranger passing us on the street prompted to say something to us we didn't expect to hear that day. It might even just be a tiny little feeling we might be inclined to ignore because it's so subtle.

God knew all life would be destroyed except for the lives on that ark. That means God already knew their hearts, he knew their intentions, and he knew the condition of incorruption of their flesh. God had allowed people to exercise their agency, hoping and giving every last opportunity for his children to turn around and make better choices to the very last opportunity possible because he loves us all so much.

I can well imagine the desperation Noah must have felt, the burden on his shoulders to make all the necessary preparations as quickly as possible, feeling time running out. I bet he worried he might not be living up to the expected standard and wondering if he was going to end up pleasing God with his finished product. But God loves effort. He loves effort and he loves us doing the best that we can. He knows our limitations and abilities even better than we do.

If the people had stopped breaking his laws and hurting one another so badly and to such a great extent, perhaps this deadly flood wouldn't have come about. Maybe it still would have happened, but what if there had been the option of having more arks because there were more incorrupt people?

The flood, the building of the ark, and living in it with the animals for over five months was a test of faith, an act of trust, and a learning experience all rolled into one. What is our flood? What is our ark? Where is our lesson? Each one of us has one. We only need look carefully at our lives, and we can see where God is directing us to save ourselves in our personal waters.

Another final destruction is coming to us in our day. This time will not be by flood of water due to a promise God made to Noah's father, Enoch. He showed Enoch in a dream what he was going to do with the flood in many future generations, and Enoch wept and pleaded in such despair that God could not deny him his request.

Enoch was so despairing to see his descendants utterly destroyed that God promised there would always be at least *some* of his posterity in all the lands of the earth. He then later made this same covenant with Noah before the flood that there would *always* be at least *some* of his posterity on the earth.

The destruction that is coming to us if we are not successful in turning ourselves around is going to be one by fire. Some might wonder if it might not be a fire of the spirit instead of a burning fire but if Noah's experience teaches us one thing, that flood was literal. The archeological evidence we have available to us today proves that it was and scientists continue to discover more and more the things that were going on during that time. So, we can only assume literal fire awaits us. You know what's good for putting out a fire?

Water.

You know where you can get some? From the fountain of living water, of course! If you're finding that your soul is parched, it's time to get hydrated and there's no time like the present. If you haven't got the fountain of living water in your soul, you won't know what metaphorical ark you will need to build to survive your flood – or your *fire,* as the case may be. There is still time but get started on it.

Did you know that the name Noah comes from the Hebrew *noach,* which means "to rest"? After Noah and his family descended out of the ark onto dry land, they built an altar and gave thanks to God for preserving them and then they rested a bit. Over five months locked up in a stuffy ark must have been quite a trial for everyone. The really neat thing is that after we go through a trial and get out on the other side, we always get a chance to rest before we begin the next thing.

Noah is known as the patriarch who survived the flood. What are you known for surviving so far in your life? There must be a list of things. And for each one of those things the fountain can cleanse and purify your body, mind, and soul until the suffering becomes a distant memory without the pain.

There can be no coincidence that the Lord used water to cleanse the earth, kind of like a baptism of sorts. We know that there must first be a baptism of water for the body. We need to baptize our internal deserts, the places of deficiency or lack of goodness in our lives, and our sadness. It is not enough to drip just a few drops of living water.

We must fully immerse ourselves in much the same way the Savior did. He chose a river that was moving, not stagnant, that could carry away all the undesirable thoughts, acts, and feelings. We must seek out those who are experts, trained and authorized to help us. And if we do, we too can have new life.

I remember a time in my life I thought I would die of metaphorical thirst, even though I was going through the motions of reading my scriptures and going to church, saying lots of prayers, and begging the Lord to release me from my emotional prison. Everyone thought I was fine because that was what they were supposed to think, but there were some who were more observant who could tell I was really struggling but no one really knew what to do other than to notice.

In Noah's time, things were so filled with darkness and wickedness that people didn't care who saw anymore. They didn't care if they did everything evilly, right out in the open and in front of everyone's faces because there were no more consequences. No keeping of the laws anymore. And they didn't care what they did to other people either. They loved themselves first and foremost before anyone else. There was no room for anyone else.

The worse things they did against someone else, the better, in their opinion. No one cared anymore. And no one did anything. And that's when people get in trouble when they stop caring about anything anymore. One person can effect a change but it takes a group of people to stand up together and say enough is enough and start holding consequences accountable and keeping and upholding the laws especially even if *and* when it hurts.

We have to be very careful. It is so easy to fall into this trap with ourselves because we falsely believe no one can see the pain and hurt that we cause ourselves internally with our thoughts, our actions, and our self-talk. We can easily fall into hurting ourselves more and more as we become accustomed to beating ourselves up and having to resort to upping the level of pain we think we must inflict upon ourselves to have the same effect as before.

If we want to stop the darkness from taking over our personal planet, resulting in a complete wipeout, we have to be willing to follow all the true laws. For each law we live, we win the positive consequences of in our life. And to do that we need to start where we are, doing the things we can today and working our way up to other things that today may look too difficult or even unsavory. Remember, oftentimes things look different when you look at them from new, higher perspectives.

We have to keep God's natural laws if we want natural benefits. We have to start with hydrating ourselves – spiritually, physically, and emotionally. There are people who don't want to change and who don't want to get better and that's okay. They are eventually on a direct flight to emotional destruction and they just may want to take as many people with them as they can right now with where they are in their life experiences. Sometimes people truly don't realize what they are doing, and if they did they never would do it.

I never would have believed when I was a young girl that I would ever live to see a day where people are afraid to leave their houses, to go to the grocery store to buy food and other necessities, to even visit a family member or visit with a neighbor. The possibility that people would be working so hard at destroying each other on social media, in the streets, in towns across this nation never occurred to me as the remotest of possibilities. I was sure I would be long gone before any of these types of things would happen among people I know and love.

Yet here we are, together, doing our best to take one step at a time, like Noah, to clean things up first within ourselves, and then helping those around us as we go. All it takes is a little sweep here, a shovel moved to a wheelbarrow there, a smile, a helping hand from me to you and from you to me.

In the meantime, people are dying of thirst now, I am, and you are. We are in a massive drought, literally and metaphorically, and people need to know where to find the fountain of water of life. We need to know how to use it: drink it in and hydrate our physical cells so our bodies can perform all the functions they need to carry out to feed us, give us energy for our activities and work, and help us to feel and look better too.

Fountain of Water of Life

People need to know how to cleanse with the living water through proper bathing, to renew our skin and balance organs, center our thoughts and feelings, and rejuvenate our spirits. And people need to understand how to use the water to restore all old things back to a new condition so they are as good or better than they ever were before the metaphorical drought.

Once everyone knows that they can drink from this never-ending fountain and cleanse their thirst and start partaking of it, everything can change. They need to know it will never run out and they can drink as long and as deeply as they want. Like Noah, first comes the notification, then comes the action and follow through, and at the end comes the blessings.

PART II
SAVING

THE WORD *SAVING* IS AN AMAZINGLY versatile word. It sadly has gained such a falsely negative connotation by those who do not understand the way it works, what it is, and what it gives you. I do love the meaning of words. Even more, I love diving deeply into every little bit about it as well.

You can learn a lot about a word you had no idea about before, like tasting a really well-made cheesecake baked from scratch for the very first time. The meanings can tell us so much about things that maybe we may not have thought otherwise, and they can give us new perspectives sometimes too.

Merriam-Webster's Dictionary defines *saving* as: preservation from danger or destruction: deliverance. In relation to hydration, it's most obvious that if we are not getting enough hydration in our life, whether it's physical, mental or emotional, or spiritual, our lives will definitely be in danger and in need of some deliverance whether it's with an I.V. from the hospital, a counselor, or a preacher.

Britannica's definition relating to saving in regards to economics is: the extent to which individuals save is affected by their preferences for future over present consumption, their future income, and to some extent by the rate of interest. When you apply that to health and hydration, you can come up with some pretty neat connections.

Are we interested in saving our health; and if so, just *how* interested are we and how much are we willing to invest our preferences to reach our intended target goal? Maybe we want to restore our inner child.

Sometimes the greater the danger or destruction, the greater our interest becomes. What are things that we value enough to preserve them? You can save a half-eaten sandwich but how much value would that have for you?

Making sure we spend our time and effort on the things that really matter the most to us and making every bit of that energy count for something helps us in the long run. We get to choose how important something is to us in any given moment and how much we want to dedicate to results.

The opposite of saving is spending. In the perspective of our best good, what are we spending our health on? If health was a form of currency, would you be a spender or a saver? You need look no further than your current state of health to know. The body doesn't lie about that.

Are we spending it in a deficit of sleep-deprived nights, highly processed sugary or strong drinks that rob us of vital nutrients or even not drinking enough of anything, and excessive lifestyle habits? Are we recklessly racking debt clear up to our ears, health-wise?

You might be a saver. You are paying attention to the things going on around you and making very conscious choices about what you take into your body, this precious temple of yours. You make sure what you drink is clean, nourishing, and pure. You know that drinking the wrong things and using filthy water will damage you.

It is so important to know the value of things. If you don't, you can't appreciate what you have until it is gone. Sometimes with our health we can find this out too late. If you value something – whether it be your chastity, your soul, or your car – you do research on its value.

You will be interested enough to find out how to best take care of what you value, to maintain it in pristine condition. It brings you great joy because you have invested in it and spent time on it. Taking steps for added care, you learn what can damage or harm your precious item or virtue and figure out ways to stay as far away from those people or things as possible. You might even set up some alarms, security, or guards to help you do this.

Learning the rules of engagement in relation to tending something can go a long way in saving just about anything from destruction or danger. So

Fountain of Water of Life

protect and save your health as fiercely as you
would your child, your favorite pet, or your donkey.
Your health is just as important, if not perhaps
maybe even more so. Without it you have nothing,
but with it you have everything.

SECTION 1
A Coat

THE TIME IS RUNNING OUT to take advantage of the cleansing fountain of living water. As we know from the record found in Genesis, [16] from the time it started to rain and the fountains of the deep broke up, it only took seven days or so for the waters of the flood to completely cover the entire earth.

For those of us familiar with localized flooding due to rain, hurricanes, tornados, or even tsunamis, we know just how quickly an inch of water can become feet within just a few seconds and miles within just a few minutes. Add to that the fountains bursting open from the deep as wide as shopping center malls and small cities across the planet. It wouldn't take more than a week to flood everything high enough for it to take one hundred fifty days for everything soak back into the ground and run off the land back into the oceans and underground.

One hundred fifty days is 5.2 months for all the waters to go back to where they were. I imagine with all the dirt and debris that got kicked up they must have plugged a lot of those fountains opening back up again as we see them today. It would be like waiting for a giant clogged bathtub to drain. It must have seemed to take forever.

God loves effort. Since he truly knows our hearts, he even knows when we're sincere or if we are just going through the motions of something, even we're only trying to fool ourselves. He rewards us for trying our best. However, he doesn't just give things to us because he's much nicer to us than to do that to us. We still have to work for things.

I have a friend whose son snuck out of the house on his motor bike with a friend. I don't think he had a helmet on. He was just a young teenager at the time. He was crossing at an intersection having the right of way, when a big old car came barreling around the corner. Being dark outside, the driver couldn't see well, and also being in a hurry, he didn't take time to really look at who or what was there. The man must have figured that everyone was already home that late at night. He hit the boy and his friend hard enough that it dented the front of the car.

The boy's friend who came along for the ride went flying off onto the road. My friend's son, calculating the rotation of his fall, realized he was going to land smack on top of his head and most likely die. At the last second, after doing all else in his power to correct his course and knowing it wasn't going to be enough, he felt an angelic hand on the back of his neck. It flipped him just enough so he didn't hit his head at all and instead landed safely on the pavement. He was able to stand and walk around.

Later that night when he was talking to his mother, he told her that he felt very strongly that God had sent his deceased, angel grandfather to watch over him that evening. His grandfather used to love riding motorcycles too. We never know how or when God will answer our prayers. Don't underestimate that the challenges and trials you're going through now might hold significant value to someone else down the road. Your story might be part of someone else's deliverance.

God does not waste our pain. Does it make him sad when bad things happen to us? Of course! He weeps with and for us. He was so upset he warned the flood would come and wipe out everything but those who were on the ark. Why doesn't he stop and rescue us out of every bad thing? Is it because he doesn't exist? No! Is it because he doesn't love us? No!

We have to recall back to the time of the pre-existence or our spirit life before we came to get a body here on earth. We lived with God. We wanted to become just like God. So he said, "Well, if you're really sure, we can put together this test run for you, and you can prove to yourself that you will still follow all the laws of truth, light, and righteousness even when you are not in my presence. And to make the test fair, we'll put the veil of forgetfulness over everyone's minds so no one remembers what being with us is like."

We would have to learn and experience the law of opposition and show that we would use our agency to choose rightly. One third of us chose for various reasons not to come and participate in this opportunity. Those who did not agree with God's plan, by their own choice work very hard to try to trip up the rest of us so we cannot succeed. They wanted to follow Satan's plan, to take away everyone's agency and force everyone to be good and force everyone to make it back so no one would be lost. It would invalidate our chance to learn how to use agency, though. And God said, "No." That was not his perfect plan, his better plan.

Being so angry they did not get their way, they try to get everyone else to do as many bad things as possible and destroy the plan. They believe the worse things you do that are against God's perfect plan for our eternal joy and happiness the better. Some of those who chose not to follow even *pretended* to be on God's side so they could come and cause worse problems for everyone here physically. We *still* wanted to come. The final end reward must be pretty worth it to us if we still came knowing all that would be stacked against us. Did we know what it was going to be like? How could we when we had no experience with our body yet?

Joseph was a very young man of seventeen years of age from a large family living in Canaan. Being that his father was so old when he had him his father really favored him and outwardly loved him more than all his other children. After tattling on his brothers – probably frequently – they got really mad at him. They finally got to the point that they plotted to kill him but one of the brothers felt too guilty about it and convinced them to sell him as a slave to the Ishmaelites instead. So they tore up Joseph's long coat, a special gift from his father, covered it with goat's blood, and told their father an evil beast had devoured Joseph.

Even though he was sold as a slave and had to endure the hardships that go along with that, the Lord helped and prospered him, eventually putting him into an influential household where his master recognized he was responsible and good with numbers. He soon gave Joseph charge over everything he owned. While Potiphar was away on business one day, Potiphar's wife tried to tempt and lie with Joseph and have inappropriate relations with him, but Joseph ran away with nothing but his integrity to cover him. Standing with his garment in her hand, Mrs. Potiphar made up a story to get revenge on Joseph, telling the other male servants there that it was Joseph who had tried to lay with *her*. Potiphar had Joseph thrown in jail, of course, and refused to believe his story.

The jailers, seeing how good Joseph was with the other prisoners and how much they respected him (because he treated everyone with the same level of respect), gave him more responsibility in the jail until he was practically running the place. While he was there, the head baker and the head butler both got thrown in jail by the Pharaoh. They both had dreams during the night and, seeing that they were sad, Joseph asked them to tell him the dreams the next morning. They were grieved because there weren't any dream interpreters in the jail, but Joseph told them interpretations belong to God. He asked them to tell him the dreams.

Joseph interpreted that in three days, the baker would be found innocent and set free. Joseph asked him to remember him kindly when he got out and ask Pharaoh to bring him out of the jail house. He told him what happened to him from his brother's throwing him in the pit, about Potiphar's wife, and up to then. The baker told him that he would remember him. Then Joseph interpreted the butler's dream as well: in three days he would be released from the jail as well but he would be found guilty and hanged from a tree.

The baker *did* remember Joseph after he was released, but not right away. It wasn't until the Pharaoh had some really bad dreams and no one could make sense of them that he did. The baker suggested they call in Joseph to interpret and told how he had interpreted his dream and the butler's. After interpreting that there would be seven years of plenty in the land followed by seven years of famine, the Pharaoh decided, after some thought, to put Joseph in charge of a plan to store up grain against the famine in order to get Egypt through. In all the land, only Pharaoh would be higher in rank than he.

The famine came after the seven years of plenty, as foretold, and word reached Joseph's family all the way in Canaan that somehow Egypt had grain to sell. His father was now too old to travel, so he sent his sons with the funds to buy some grain for them and then return. They had no idea that the brother they had sold was there and in charge!

When Joseph recognized his brothers, he tested them to see if their hearts had changed towards him at all. He wanted to give them a chance to confess the guilt of what they had done without knowing it was him to see if they were truly sorry and not just willing to say anything only to get grain. He made them relive a similar pattern of what they did to him but disguised in a different way.

Joseph finally revealed himself to them as their brother after many trials and hardships imposed upon them. Once he finally revealed himself to them for who he was, he told them not to be sad or angry with themselves for what they had done to him. He said:

"And God sent me before you to preserve you a posterity in the earth and to save your lives by a great deliverance." [17]

Joseph's pain was not wasted, his sorrows were put to very good use, and his healing complete enough that he could see God's mercy in helping him wind up where he most needed to be when he most needed to be there. Because of what he was able to endure, he was able to help a lot of people that he might not have been able to had he remained at home with his family.

There are many others lives at varying levels and areas of influence whose paths have followed similar patterns. The biggest example is Christ. On a more personal note, maybe someone in your family has been an example of deliverance in one way or another. The thing about deliverance is it doesn't usually happen immediately, when we want it to, or in the way we expect.

God's timetable is different than ours. His calendar is different than the Gregorian calendar that a lot of the world uses now. His timing is perfect. Often there are layers we never could have anticipated and the involvement of layers we never could have dreamed of and the involvement of things we'd never think of. The wonder and working of his design are truly miraculous. Every part and piece must be in place before it happens.

There are many things we do not understand about God's timing. One thing we cannot see is all the other people who are involved. Another thing we are not aware of is all the resources required. We do not hear all the prayers sent up for the same deliverance. All the levels of salvation that are offered to us along with our deliverance are unfathomable.

Did you know, God started preparing for our deliverance before the request ever came out of our mouths? He knew before we ever got into the situation that we would need saving. He knew who would need our help and who would benefit from our trials. Most importantly, he knew how they would benefit *us* too, as painful as it might be.

Now, I'm not saying God condones bad things. He's made it quite clear that he doesn't. He just takes our pain – working within the gift of each individual's agency – transforms it into an oasis where a desert used to be, and heals our minds and hearts.

Kindness is a great salve during healing times. An appreciative word, a gentle touch, an act of service, a note of appreciation, or little gifts are all appropriate ways to help lift someone's spirit who may be tired after a long day's work, a secretly challenging time in their life, or overbearing sorrows weighting on their shoulders. Sometimes people going through a healing crisis struggle to put on their happy smiling faces.

Sojourning in the wilderness, the Israelites were sad, afraid, and lonely for home. Even though the Egyptians treated them cruelly, it was familiar. It was in their DNA. The memory of generations of slavery got stored away in the body. Traditions were born out of their slavery and shared until it was natural to copy, paste, and repeat. As they charted more and more unfamiliar territory, their brains screamed at them to go back to the old life. They begged to return to the familiarity of their food. They did not care that they would be beaten every day and that many of them would die.

Our bodies play the same panicking trick on us as we start to really heal ourselves. As we go out into what seems a barren, empty wasteland, we fear the change, the hiding, and the truth. We must resist this natural tendency to panic and run away with everything in us over and over if we are to see different results. *Everything* we think and do matters.

Separate details and events led up to the liberation of Israel from Egypt. At the time, I'm sure they never would have imagined a slave giving birth to a son, destined to be murdered for merely being born a male, would not be able to bear the thought of her newborn son's death. They couldn't have foreseen her family's plan to hide him in a basket in the river would wind up floating in to Pharaoh's sister's view as she was out wading. That Pharaoh's sister, being barren, would save the babe, seeing the gods had seen fit to save his life. He would be nursed by his own birth mother and raised in royalty where he would learn everything he would later need to know to confront his now adopted cousin.

Who knew Moses's relationship with his biological family would help him understand the worth of a soul? And who knew that he would stand up to a guard for senselessly beating an elderly slave, and end up accidentally killing the guard? How could anyone have known that this event would cause Moses to run away into the desert where he would see God in a burning bush?

God would call Moses to free his people and teach him how to do it. Could anyone know Moses would go back to Egypt, confront the new Pharaoh, his adopted cousin? After much stubbornness, being shown forth God's power through multiple miracles, resulting in the death of his own son, Pharaoh finally let the people go. The people of Egypt even bestowed riches on them so they could afford to leave. In fact, they *begged* them to go!

"Thus the Lord saved Israel that day out of the hand of the Egyptians." [18]

There are multiple instances of the Lord doing similar types of deliverance in other places, in different ways. An ancient people in North America, known today as the Adenas, have a written record as well, of having been captured and enslaved by their enemies for years. Their enemies tricked them into giving up their liberty, thinking it was for a good reason. Instead, they found themselves getting into a deeper hole that they could not get out of their own, enslaved and in over their heads.

Many of the Adena people died trying to escape by their own power on various occasions with no luck. They couldn't even get word out to bring help back! There's a lot more to the story, but in the same kind of timing, the Lord sent a deliverer amongst them and over the Passover holiday, they made ready to escape, this time on the Lord's command and in his timing. Now their story has become an inspiration of deliverance to many.

They got the guards really drunk as part of their escape, and then all slipped out the back gate and miraculously through a narrow pass in the cool of the night that happens to this day to be famously overrun by tens of thousands of poisonous snakes. The next day when the guards awoke to find all their slaves gone, they pursued mightily but were not able to follow due to all the many serpents out sunning themselves! The people were able to reunite safely in another city with their old friends and family they hadn't seen in ages. It had been so long that their families had wondered if they were even still alive. They all rejoiced together, being reunited once again.

There are many other similar stories where God has delivered his people in his proper timing by miraculous means that have been stuck in more than humble circumstances. He knows who is ready, and he knows when the right time is, as we've seen with the Israelites and the Adena.

Fountain of Water of Life

SECTION 2
Deliverance

SECTION 2

Deliverance

A PERFECT EXAMPLE OF GOD'S deliverance involved a guy named Gideon. Israel found themselves, once again in captivity, this time to the Midianites. Midian was located in what is now known as the northwest Arabian Peninsula on the east shore of Aqaba on the Red Sea. Israel had been their captive for a long time and they were getting to the point where they really weren't too happy about it.

Gideon was central to the plan of Israel's deliverance, but he was not the main key. He was not the starring role in the story. God got that role. Things were pretty tough for Israel. If you can imagine, they had to resort to making themselves dens in caves and in the mountains because every time harvest time came, other people came and destroyed all their crops until there was nothing left.

Push came to shove, and there was a big upset. A bunch of people sided with Gideon to prepare for battle to free the people from the Midianites. God told him he had too many guys volunteering for the job. He told Gideon that if he went up with that many men, the men would just get all puffed up in their own pride and say that they themselves won the battle alone and would not acknowledge the Lord's hand in it.

God told Gideon to go and tell these men who had come to fight in battle that whoever was afraid and fearful should leave. Having heard this statement, twenty-two thousand men left and there were only ten thousand of them still there.

God then told Gideon that there were still too many people there. He told Gideon to take the men to the water and that he should test them. God said, whoever I tell you, you will not take them with you to battle. The test was that he should watch and see which men would scoop the water in their hand up to their mouth and which ones would bow down on their knees like dogs when getting a drink. Those that would scoop the water were the ones he would take with him. There were only three hundred men that scooped up the water in their hands. The rest were sent home.

The Lord said to Gideon, "By the three hundred men that lapped will I save you and deliver the Midianites into your hand."[19] They gave some food to the rest of the men who the Lord did not qualify and sent them home. He then told Gideon to go and take his servant Phurah with him and sneak down to the Midianite camp that night.

The Midianite army was so large in number they were like multitudes of grasshoppers upon the land and whose camels alone were in number like the sands of the sea. God wanted Gideon to listen to how he was delivering Midian into Gideon's hands. What he ended up hearing would help

Gideon have confidence in God's ability to deliver them.

Once Gideon and Phurah snuck down to the camp, they heard a man who came to share a dream he had. He said that a cake of barley bread tumbled into their midst to a tent. It smote the tent so hard it fell and overturned it so that it was now flat. Another Midian man interpreted the dream for him. He said that there was nothing else this dream could mean but the sword of Gideon, who was the son of Joash, and a man of Israel. He continued, saying that God had delivered Midian into Gideon's hand and all of the Midian army along with it.

Gideon praised God and went back to the host of Israel and told them to get up, that God had delivered Midian into their hands. The men followed the directions Gideon gave them, which terrified the Midianites, who ran, cried, and fled from them. Israel pursued the Midianites and conquered.

Some takeaways from this bit of history are that no matter how overwhelming the odds may seem to be against you, no matter how powerful your enemy may appear to be (including how our own mental, emotional, spiritual obstacles appear to be), and no matter how scared you might be to move forward, with God's support, you can do all things he tells you to do.

We can overcome, and we can conquer. All it takes is a few seconds of courage to take action. All these examples show us that it is not enough to just pray for his help, although that can be a great start. Always pray for his help and his guidance, and *then* you *must* take action. Figure out what the first step is and make sure it's in the right direction.

If you feel peace about it, not confusion, then it's right. Study it out in your mind first. We live in a day where truth is called lies and lies are truth. Light is darkness and darkness is light. It is done so blatantly and obviously that many are confused and don't know who or what to believe. Study out laws of universal truth, not man's knowledge, so you know what they are and will not be deceived.

This can be our own thoughts we believe about ours or someone else's beliefs we've decided to adopt as our own. The things we think or hear or the negative pressure from others who may or may not think they have your best interests at heart can become jail cells within our own minds. Though the prison bars are gone we don't realize how easily we could be free simply because we can't see the bars are no longer there! Our abuser may be gone and we might have picked up where they left off, beating and bruising ourselves far more than they ever could.

A little water applied to the wound can soothe the trouble away.

There was a great and mighty king whose fame was spread throughout all nations. He was King David of Israel. He had reclaimed the Ark of the Covenant, and the people all united in one heart under him as he was made king. The Philistines were not happy to hear about it and came up against him twice, but God delivered them into King David's hands both times.

David then prepared the temple where the ark would be housed. Appointed by the authority of God, the Levites had been selected to be the only ones to carry the ark. They were called and anointed for their calling and then they prepared for a feast of thanksgiving to the Lord for delivering them out of the hands of their enemies. It is in a psalm that David wrote that the steps of deliverance are given to us:

"And say, Save us, O God of our Salvation, and gather us together, and deliver us from the heathen, that we may give thanks to thy holy name, and glory in thy praise." [20]

After we ask God to save us or help us, which is the first step, we ask him to gather us. Our first natural instinct, whether we believe in him or not, is to cry out for help. Our heart cries for saving or deliverance does it not? "Please help me out of this _____ situation!"

Second, we want to feel safe, protected from the hurt, the fear, and whatever is causing us pain. If we've been separated from our loved ones in the process, we want to be reunited with them, whole and sound again. It may even be that we want to have the shattered pieces of ourselves put back together.

Naturally (and thirdly), we want to be as far away from the person or people who hurt us and for justice to be done to them for what they did to us. Regardless of when and how God choses to mete that out on them we must move forward with mercy for ourselves and our own healing.

The fourth and most important (but often overlooked) step is remembering to be grateful for the deliverance we receive. Not only do we remember but we express it and also give the glory to God. Without him we really can't do much. With his help we can see and be witness to miracles in our lives.

SECTION 3

Contrite Spirit, Consequences, and Revenge

WE LOOK AROUND AND SEE OR HEAR of other people who have asked for and received help. What's the difference that they got help right away and someone else did not? It doesn't seem fair or just, does it? Doesn't God make sure everything is exactly the same for everyone so things can be equal for everyone? If God is perfect, wouldn't he make everyone perfectly happy and healthy all the time? *Bless me* if *I* think I'm good and *curse* someone else if *I* think they are wicked or sinful!

God doesn't work that way. That's the imperfect, misunderstanding man trying to remove all pain and responsibility for the consequences of every single person's actions. The ego tries to make us think we need to remove all trace of mortal frailties and imperfections. It's a lot of noise trying to cover up the discomfort of our own brokenness. God follows universal laws and he knows he needs to teach us how to understand them. He does this by giving us his word and by sending his son to be a living example to us in this life.

As we do our best to listen to his word and follow his promptings, he is quick to hear us and answer our prayers. The answer may not always be what we want to hear, but answer us he does. There are songs and books written on the subject like "Sometimes the Answer is No" (by Samuel Lloyd Shelby) or even not right now, or it depends do what you like.

Sometimes we aren't clear on what it is that we really want, so we need to take care of that first before asking, so we can get a straight answer to our question. Try to make it a yes or no question so you can get a clear answer. We should not put ourselves in the assumption or habit of expecting God to do all the work or even all the thinking for us! We are here to learn to become more like him, so some action is required on our part.

We must learn how to work then. Part of working is learning how to reason things out and how to do research, *real* research. If everything was always handed to us on a silver platter, we'd become weak and apathetic. We would never learn how to do anything ourselves, and we'd not be very good use to anyone, including to ourselves. We'd never learn compassion or gratitude. We'd never grow to become great, as God has in store for us.

King David had a way with words. He had a knack for writing psalms, and he wrote a lot of them. One of his favorite things to write about was God and his nature. One of his psalms contains the answer to the question "Who does God listen to the most?" David wrote:

"The Lord is nigh (or near) unto them that are of a broken heart; and saveth such as be of a contrite spirit." [21]

Now, a broken heart, most of us can relate to in some form or another with what that must feel like. Many of us have had our hearts broken many times. I'm not referring to merely the romantic kind of broken heart. There are lots of ways a heart can be broken: things that make us feel unloved can be listed on into eternity alone.

What is a *contrite* spirit? In the Hebrew language it means to be crushed in spirit. It takes a great amount of opposition or force to crush something. This means to be humbled, full of regret or remorse for what you've done. It means to see the error of your ways and want true forgiveness. It means being a penitent man.

It can be really easy to get caught up going from feeling the grief of the consequences of our own actions based on things that broke our hearts to feeling anger and the need for revenge. In our culture it is frowned upon, sadly, to be sad. We are rewarded and praised, on the other hand, for being angry instead. Attitudes of vengeance, revenge, the phrase "I don't get mad; I get ahead" are falsely glorified. This erroneously leads people down a dark path out of which they will have a difficult time pulling themselves. It becomes like something called a maelstrom.

A maelstrom is a very powerful whirlpool so strong that is can suck in all vessels into it, even the largest and most powerful of ships. Maelstroms are so strong that anything coming within a wide radius is still pulled in. The term extends to any great turmoil that relentlessly drags men into it. We see time and again where there is revenge taken by one side, that there must be retribution in kind by the other, and then more revenge. It never stops. Each act draws in more people: entire families, communities, and nations.

This is not the way to healing. This is not the way to peace. And this is not the way back to find love. It is the way to greater and hotter hate – and death. In this space, you can never live and you can never have peace, love, or prosperity. Soon you forget the reason for the pain and the addition of more pain *to* the pain is that is all there seems to be left there. To feed it, you must cause more and more pain. But that is not the way to get to what you truly desire. It is nothing but a false and empty hope. Feed emptiness with emptiness and what you end up with is just a lot more emptiness. This can never wash away your pain, guilt, or remorse.

It's a 180-degree turn-around that can get you out of a pain cycle, and it's the only way. And it is when we are stuck in a big maelstrom that we definitely need God's help to get ourselves out. I learned this principle as a young girl on an eddy in an inflatable raft in a pond.

An eddy is much smaller version of a whirlpool. As a child, I was told to stay away from one in a pond because it was large enough in the center to suck down the whole inflatable raft we were in to the bottom, where we would most certainly drown. It was in the very middle of the pond and the water smoothly just disappeared over the edges and down into the center. There was no circular current you could see on top of the water, and it all seemed very peaceful and still.

The pond was large enough that we could have easily had fun paddling around and while staying away from the big pipe that created this vortex in the middle of the pond. The older person in the boat with me and my younger brother, who was paddling it, decided he wanted to scare us, and so he purposely went straight out to the eddy. He had promised our father not to go over there with us, but either he didn't really mean it or perhaps he just wanted to take advantage of having a bit of fun at our expense. I'm sure he must have thought he was clever enough to get us all back out again very easily because the water looked deceptively calm.

We only narrowly escaped as our raft was soon quickly pulled over towards the center, much to our paddler's great horror. I could see he was definitely no longer in control and was unable to get us away again as part of his prank, as he had hoped. We were too small to swim ourselves or help paddle, even if there had been more than one to use and could only frantically scream for help. I was grateful my father had told me exactly what to do in the case that something like that should happen. I was able to tell the paddler what to do, and he was able to do it—barely. It took great effort on his part, so much that he was literally shaking throughout the ordeal. Thanks to fast thinking, I'm grateful to this day for the knowledge that had been given to me that it was possible to get out and how.

We don't have to wait for the wrongs against us to be righted in order to start healing. I'm pretty sure we didn't get too much of an apology for almost getting us all killed; the poor paddler was so embarrassed. We just had to forgive him for his choice of bad judgment and try to avoid him and his pranks in the future.

The fact is that no matter how much we would *like* an apology, a *sincere* one, we have been encouraged to move on without it. We are still to do all we can do to make the offense known to the one who has harmed us and not keep it to ourselves, to seek justice through a court of law where applicable, and to hope restitution will be made to us but not hold the train of our lives waiting for it. The rest of the details we leave in God's hands. Remember, he knows the best timing, all those involved, the hearts of everyone, and the whole situation. His justice is going to be much better than anything *you* could dream up to get even with them. In Proverbs it reads:

"Say not thou, I will recompense evil; but wait on the Lord, and He will save thee." [22]

What this means is: don't say you're going to get even or get retribution for what another person did to you. Instead, wait on God to finish dealing with the rest of it. Give him all your worry over it, your pain and sorrow. He can dish out what's coming far better than you can with a punishment worthy of the crime. And while your focus is on God, he is going to be healing your heart.

God's timing is also the best, and he can give the other person the best opportunity to really feel the regret and the pain that they caused you, and possibly change for the better because of it. It's one of the most merciful things he lets us all experience as part of the healing process when we've wronged someone or someone has wronged us. Without feeling the shame of what we've done, we cannot even begin the healing process.

Still, make sure that you report crimes to the judicial system that need to be reported. That's a natural part of consequences and when people choose to make bad choices, *they* have chosen the consequences they need to experience, not you. If you can do all that, then God can also save you. We must offer up our pain with willing hearts.

Nothing good comes of a maelstrom of madness. Only good can come of a contrite spirit. On the one hand, we are merely reacting, and the other, we take conscious action and effort. With one, you end up with bad results, and with the other, as they say, "good things come to those who wait." While you're waiting, make good use of your time and work on *yourself*, on healing, and on letting go. It's the higher road to take and the higher work you can and should do.

Some of the things we can do that help ourselves let go and in the self-healing process are the twelve resources in my previous book "*Member Heal Thyself*". Hydration is one of the keys we need, whether it is on the physical, spiritual, or mental and emotional level. *This* book is a more in-depth look at the first resource (hydration) than is covered in "*Member Heal Thyself*". That first book is a good overview of everything to get started, and if you haven't read it yet, I highly recommend you start with that.

Each one of these books will help you create a sturdy, solid, unbreakable foundation on which you can build your wellness mansion. The same way you build a wellness mansion, you also build a wellness person. You must start from the foundation, the feet up. With each new level you gain a new addition to your house. Eventually, you have the full person. Not just a full person but a *whole* one.

If you are whole and strong, you will be able to stand taller and stronger. There will be no more stooping over in grief and pain. There is a beautiful passage from Proverbs that says:

"Whoso walketh uprightly shall be saved..."[23]

There are so many meanings to this verse. In a physical sense, walking upright could be referring to using our muscles in the most effective way. Using good posture is essential so we don't wear out our joints and so our organs can function properly. This saves us a lot of physical problems in the long run.

If we consider the mental and emotional aspects of walking upright, we may think about keeping the mind in check and balancing high and low feelings. We all know how easily our thoughts can run away with themselves! Feeling very strong high or low emotions can affect hormones, mood, and even affect our behavior and how we treat others. These can lead us to dangerous and eventually harmful situations.

Walking upright spiritually is like walking through a forest during a warm summer rain. You can hear the gentle patter of the drops as they fall against the leaves and as they land in the soft pine needles around you. The smells of the plants rise up to greet you with each step. It's about knowing your way through as you listen for truth and follow it. Spiritual uprightness saves us from error, pain, and the salty, burning tears of sorrow.

Some would say all could be saved in these ways. I wish it were so. For it is not easy to change the way you walk, talk, dress, or think. It is not easy to act differently than you are accustomed to for the long term. And it is not easy to make a noise differently than you are used to sounding in every ear. If it were easy, everyone would be doing it, and doing it well!

There are lots of reasons for not changing. One reason is that we are comfortable where we are. Even if life is painful where we are, it's still comfortable and familiar. Another reason is that the brain is wired to resist change. If you want it, you're really going to have to work hard to change your own mind!

Time: we think we have plenty of it and we'll do it later, later, later. That "later" never comes. Money is another factor that may hold us back. We either believe we don't have enough, or we think we are the last thing worth spending our hard-earned money on. There are a lot of other reasons you can probably think of; and these are just a few of the most popular ones that I hear from patients.

You don't have to think this way and there are options out there that can work for you, if you *really* want them to. That's the biggest key to all healing. You have to *want* it or you can't truly start.

In the Book of Luke, the author tells about a time when the people were being taught by Jesus as he walked. The people had a lot of questions for him about who the bigger sinner was in a variety of scenarios. The basic gist of his sermon was: return to rightness and straightness or pay the price. He kept working his way towards Jerusalem and there was a person who asked him if there would only be a few people who would be saved:

"Then said one unto him, Lord are there few that be saved?" [24]

I'm sure many have asked that same question in their own minds. They are *sure* that they themselves will (or won't) be saved and that others won't (or that still others will). or that still others will. This may play into the mind or the heart as to why or why someone might not work towards walking upright. The belief that "I don't need it, want it, or believe in it" holds many people back. All of this is to comply with our inner stories. The vessel that breaks and is destroyed or the cresting wave of our inner maelstrom of denial is all that seems to exist.

Christ's answer to the question is very telling and honest. We can gloss over the surface of it and miss most of the message or we can take the time to break it down and digest it, bit by bit so we get the full purpose. He tells us what we must do to begin the journey. The word *strive* means, according to Merriam-Webster, to devote serious effort or energy. Dictionary.com says it means to exert oneself vigorously; to try hard.

Cambridge English Dictionary says it is to try very hard to do something or to make something happen, especially for a long time or against difficulties. And Strong's Concordance tells us the origin in Hebrew is the word *agōnizesthe* or *agōnizomai* which means to contend for a prize, to struggle, like being engaged in an intense athletic contest or in warfare.

With this in mind, Luke tells us all to "strive to enter in at the straight or narrow gate: for many, I say unto you, will seek to enter in, and shall not be able."

This applies whole heartedly to the process of self-healing. There are many who will start or want to, or even try to begin the process. A few will make it past the first appointment or two with their wellness or even medical providers. Some may even have several visits and then quit. Or they keep stopping and starting over and over, convincing themselves they're still making progress when all they're doing is repeating the same work but not getting anywhere.

Likewise, in drinking the same glass of metaphorical water over and over, you may convince yourself you've drunk hundreds of glasses. In reality you've only drunk one while your spirit is slowly dying of dehydration.

How hard are you willing to strive to reach your intended healing destination? How much strength have your mental, emotional, and spiritual muscles got to give to your fight? Are you willing to do what it takes to build up more metaphorical and literal muscle and strength as you go along so you can keep fighting when it gets unbearably hard?

It's not the muscles of the world you need for this battle. It's the internal fortitude to never give up. It means doing whatever it takes. The greatest champion isn't always the strongest. It's the one who keeps fighting to get up one more time, and one more time, and one more until he has won.

If you don't know how much reserve you have, enter the narrow gate and find out. If you want to make sure you can keep going, find someone better at staying on the path than you and team up with them. Let them teach you but do not make *them* your fountain. Learn everything you can from them and exercise those *striving* muscles.

Get your support team together and keep each other going. No one said you had to walk the path alone. In fact, though you may enter the gate by yourself you can't stay on the path without the loving, Big Guy's help. Yes, God's help, and yes, he loves you. There will be a few others also on the path. There's no rule that says you can't encourage each other. Ultimately the responsibility comes down to you, but you can't make it on your own merits. It's impossible.

There are basically only two choices. One is to enter the gate and stay on it. Hang on for dear life! It's going to be a wild ride. The other option may look like a bunch of different choices but they all boil down to not being on the path. Even if you try to enter but are not able to, you are in the group with the lot of them who didn't make it through the gate. It's a lot easier to not be on the path. You don't have to try so hard, but you don't get the prize.

The prize is pretty great, though, and very worth the effort of trying, even though we all have to keep *on* trying. In the end, you get *everything* the Father has. (Rumor has it that everything that he has is pretty spectacular.) It's so great that we cannot even begin to imagine or fathom how amazing it is that he is offering to us. We must have had an idea before we were born into this world because we opted to be here and take our best shot.

Ultimately, when it comes down to it, no one else can help you but God and yourself. So you *do* have to help yourself out. No one else can get you to the gate. There is not a single other person who can step through it for you. And there's no one who can replace you in staying on the path. Someone can *show* you the gate. They can point it out to you. That's about all they can do other than offer moral support and be your cheerleader. But you have to be willing to be your own cheerleader too.

If you want to cleanse your soul of all the past trauma and negative emotion, it's very much the same thing. You can't wait on your mom or dad to help you or pay for your therapy or treatments. You can't cover it up with drugs and expect it to just go away. A spouse can't do it; your friends, your kids, your pets won't do it for you. It's up to *you*. We are here to support you, but even if no one is, you still have to be willing to stand up and do it for yourself until the right support team comes along and God will be with you if you ask him to.

There will be a lot of crabs in your metaphorical bucket that will try to pull you back down in with them. Have you heard of crabs in a bucket? If you put a crab alone in a bucket it will easily climb out and escape. But if you put a crab in a bucket with a few of its other fellow crabs, something strange happens. One at a time as they try to climb out, the other crabs will pull them back down to their collective misery. That's why you don't need to keep a lid on a bucket of live crabs. They keep themselves all trapped in the group's terrible end. You've got to get yourself in a separate bucket from the rest.

For some reason, people are a little bit like crabs in a way. If you've noticed, when someone starts to see some success in their life, whether it's losing weight or getting ahead in life, there are some people who will step up and try to sabotage that person. If someone has something nicer than you or vice versa they will put a scratch in your car or chip that nice thing so it's not as nice anymore. It's a type of theft, really.

Thankfully, not all people are this way and have learned that one person's success is the success of us all. They know there's more than enough room for everyone to do well in one area or another and we can all eventually have nice things if we do the work to earn them.

It can be really easy to let the crabs of the world keep us down. Especially if we've been pulled down all our lives and betrayed by those around us, those who we *should* have been able to trust. As the world gets further and further down the dark road it's chosen for itself, you will see, feel, and hear more and more clamor to join them in their dark and muddy riverbeds.

Noah's day was as dark and muddy as our own today. It was a time filled with so much crookedness that God regretted ever creating man and cleansed the entire world with a great flood. In the time of Christ, on the day of Pentecost, Peter, one of the twelve apostles, was preaching to a multitude of people about these last days. He also proclaimed unto them that the Lord God had made the same Jesus that they had crucified, their Lord and Savior. He told them that Christ had been sent to save them. Christ was the *only* way by which they could be saved and healed.

Their consciences got to the people in the crowd and their hearts were pricked with the realization of what they'd done. They asked him what they should do. He told them quite a few things which basically came down to Acts 2:40:

"...saying, Save yourselves from the untoward [or crooked] generation." [25]

It seems like most people today think they are headed in a pretty straight direction if you ask them right out. But if, even back then, Peter was saying that the whole generation was untoward and crooked, is it possible that we have become so crooked we only *think* we are straight? If we could see our path and choices compared to what he considered to be straight would we be amazed by how different the two would look?

I have to shift people on the massage table all the time when they first get on before we even start, because they lay down thinking they are centered on the table and they are at an angle and tipping this way and that, compensating for injuries and tired muscles, and not even realizing it. Once I straighten them, they are shocked at how crooked they feel. Once we help reset the muscles closer to where they should be, they feel taller, lighter, and stronger!

How many of us are willing to take a good hard look at how we are doing and make necessary course adjustments as we go along? Maybe we are not strong enough to turn that wheel all the way to where our path would match God's but we can keep making little corrections until we do catch up to him.

The people, who heard Peter's words and took them to heart with gladness, went, and changed their life choices where they needed changing. They then were baptized to symbolize this death of their old lives and the rebirth into their new ones. They entered the narrow gate. They increased their vibrational frequency and healed themselves as they continued onward.

They allowed themselves to become fluid like water to change into something better, cleaner, and more whole. How is this possible that it could be so easily done? All things in nature are made of water. Plants, rocks, all creatures great and small, even this planet we call home. Without water we could never make it through this life. We rely on it for everything.

Even now we exist in water in the form of air. Just as our lungs were filled with water before we were born, in our independent bodies we breathe in a different version of water. Air, the breath of life, reminds our bodies of the constant need for cleansing and rebirth.

Water heals us, moves us forward in life, helps us to let go, and allows us to rejoice! Christ is the living water of our spirits, of our souls. What does it mean *to live*? Dictionary.com says it's a verb: "to have life, as an organism, to be alive." My favorite definition: "to be *capable* of Vital Functions: all things that Live, continue to have Life; remain alive." What are vital functions? Are yours all working properly? Are you sure? "Therefore, *living* is continuing in existence, operation, memory, etc..."

Miriam-Webster beautifully defines *living* as: "active, functioning; exhibiting the life or motion of nature: NATURAL. Full of life or *Vigor*. True to *LIFE*: vivid, suited for living. Also meaning very as in scared the living daylights out of me. The conduct or manner of life. Christ the *very* waters."

The actual Strong's Concordance definition of *living* is: "to live, breathe, be among the living. To enjoy *real* life to have true life and worthy of the name, active, blessed, endless in the kingdom of God. To live i.e., Pass life, in the manner of living and acting as in morals or character. Living Water, having vital power in itself and exerting the same upon the soul, and a metaphor to be full of vigor, to be fresh, strong, efficient, as an adjective, active, powerful efficacious." In Proverbs it reads:

"It shall be health to thy navel and marrow to thy bones." [26]

And I think it applies here to living waters as well. There are so many things I could talk about just with this one scripture but I'll try to just stick with a few things to get you thinking about hydration. When we think about the word *health,* it leads us in this context to the word *healing.* We find safety when we move towards good health.

The word *navel* is equal to our umbilical which is also figurative as the center of strength. We gain all this when we come through the living water. It binds us together. It helps us find courage to do what we needed to do all along. And it finds us filling in the holes of life that have left us wanting.

The great thing about water is that it is really good at filling in holes and empty spaces. Now, as we partake of the living waters, we find we have no more need for things of the past that no longer serve us. We leave those things behind for the better life we receive after letting go. As scary as it sounds to let go, I can tell you from experience that the more you are able to do just that, even if it's just a little bit at a time, the better you are going to start to feel.

How can we take advantage of living water; where do we begin? As was mentioned in my first book *"Member Heal Thyself"*, I talked about a triangle of healing (See Figure 1 below). At each corner there is an aspect of healing. One is spirituality. Another is mental and emotional healing. The other is physical. They are, all three, connected to each other and affected by one another.

Spiritual

Mental/Emotional   Physical

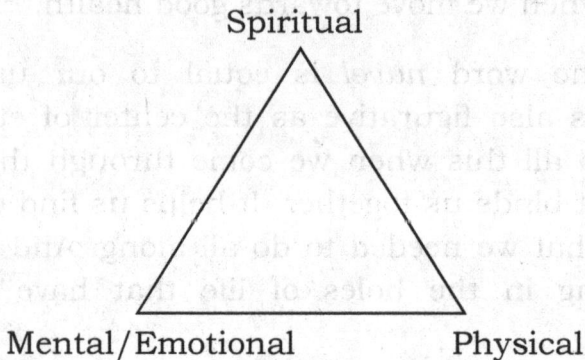

(Figure 1. Spiritual, mental/emotional, and physical pyramid for complete wellness.)

You cannot work on one without having an effect on the other two. As an example, if I do a spiritual practice like prayer, it will affect my physical health and my mental and emotional wellbeing. Vice versa, if I do something for my physical health, like eat healthy, diet, or work out, etc...that will positively affect my mood and my spirituality.

If I practice positive self-talk, meditation, and thinking kindly of myself and others, likewise, that will affect my spirituality and my physical health. One of the most important things to know about this triangle is that the most powerful transformations occur when we start with the spiritual corner first.

When you go to create something, whether you build a building, bake some bread, or start a business, it has to start with something of true substance. It has to begin with a spark of life. It then becomes a thought or idea. Finally, it takes on shape and form. Raising our health vibration is no different. We start with our spiritual lives. That trickles to our thinking and feeling, which then flows to our physical health. That is the secret to permanent, lasting change. Nothing else can replace it. It is the full, correct, and true way to get to where you want to be.

Where do you begin? This entire book has been pointing you to the first corner of the healing triangle. Immerse yourself in God and his plan for you in your life. Rely wholly on him to guide you and lead you in what you should do. *Ask* him to guide you. He can and will show you who can help you *if* you let him. Trust him to help you. Despite all that any of us have experienced, thinking that maybe he doesn't love or care about us individually for whatever reason, we *can* rely on him. I have finally learned for myself; that it is a fact. It takes time to work through our perceptions to get to the point where we can believe it, but it is there. It's real and it's true.

SECTION 4
Cleansing

Fountain of Water of Life

IN MY WELLNESS NEWSLETTER I give you tips to help you drink more water. I share hydrating water recipes, ideas, and resources to help you get excited about how to get more good water physically inside of you. However, these tips will only help if you understand the process and the triangle of healing in the last section. You may feel better being more hydrated, but without the spiritual aspect, you'll miss out on the biggest part of the full cleansing power of water. You are welcome to join the newsletter if you'd like extra ideas not included in this book. You'll find the website at the end.

What I will be including in this book are some ideas for a combination of mental/emotional and physical bathing practices, but you should also research separately into and contemplate the spiritual aspect of it as well. The skin is our largest organ and is vital for a majority of our nutrient intake. Many people are unfamiliar with this information, and that's why it's so important.

We should also be so careful about the products we put on our skin. Toxic chemicals we smell or apply to the skin can be found in the brain within mere seconds! That's not good for the brain and may cause damage. This amazing, protective outer layer of our body – the skin – can bring nutrients in through it and release all the gross garbage out of it. Likewise, it can soak up toxic chemicals from our environment, which is why we need clean air and natural scents so much.

Bathing over showering gives the opportunity to take in nutrients and release garbage. Yes, while showering *is* quick and efficient, it is not always sufficient. Even for adults, bathing at minimum once a week is highly recommended. Not only for the nutritional benefits but also for cleansing pores, hydrating, healing, and for helping our organs to balance out any little things that become riddled with knots and energetic blockages. Bathing also helps to clear up emotional trappings and is a wonderful way to practice self-love and care.

I know it can be difficult for many of us to get ourselves into a bath in the first place. For some it is even a physical complication. If you do have a health condition that prevents you from bathing yourself fully, think about starting with foot-baths. You can do them at home inexpensively or go to a place that offers that service to you. There are ionic foot baths, mud footbaths, and more.

For baths, fifteen to twenty minutes is a general good rule of thumb. For about ten minutes the body absorbs moisture and nutrients from the bath and the next ten is spent releasing garbage back out into it. The body starts reabsorbing again after about twenty minutes and so it's a really good idea to make sure you get out of the water by that time. You don't want to reabsorb all the garbage back into yourself that you just released. It's plenty of time to soften up the dead skin that needs to be scrubbed and sloughed off too and invigorate the lymph nodes, which help clean the body.

You may have heard of the Sedona, Arizona, vortexes. They are actually quite famous. If you've been there and felt how powerful they are, you know they are real. There are similar things that are part of the human body, just as palpable, just smaller in nature. If you have not have heard of them it's okay. I had not until I had moved here. Or if I had, they weren't on my radar at the time and so I didn't really pay them much attention then. For those not familiar with what a vortex is, I will explain a little. Even if you are acquainted, you may learn something new.

A vortex is a physics phenomenon. It happens when you have liquid or a gas that is moving in rotating circles. In the center you have what is called a vortex line that the liquid or gas swirls around. The vortex forms when there is a difference in the rate of speed at which the matter swirls around the vortex line. You may be more familiar with the examples of hurricanes, tornadoes, and whirlpools or eddies.

A manmade example would be how the air moves over an airplane wing. The vortexes of the planet are at the intersections of the natural electromagnetic earth energy, also known as lay lines. Perhaps you have seen trees twisted that are not a naturally twisted type of tree. These indicate that vortex energy is present.

On the body you also have vortexes in various places. The largest and main ones are located down the center of the body. There are seven of them with the first starting between the legs at the root and moving up to the crown of the head. Each has been found to have different properties and responsibilities.

When they're not rotating freely and openly, they create imbalances and, likewise, when imbalances are created, they cause problems with the vortex movements and rotations. We can use bathing not only to nourish our body but also to restore balance to the vortexes in the body. You can try each one out at a time starting from the base, or root, and working your way up to the top of the head for best results.

Bath Balancing

Directions: Run a warm bath. Add your choice of herbal tea, gem or gems (making sure they are water safe!), and if desired, essential oils to the bath. Once you add your items to the water take a beautiful photo and post it on your social media, if you like, and encourage others to enjoy a balancing bath.

If you feel like it, you may tag me on Instagram @MemberHealThyself and use the hashtag #memberhealthyself or on Facebook at @RebeccaSheltonAuthor on Facebook and use the hashtags #fountainoflivingwater or #flwbaths. Our favorite photos will be featured on our pages.

NOTE: Do not use any of the items if you have a known sensitivity or allergy to the teas, essential oils, or the gem-stones. Consult your medical doctor if you have any medical conditions to make sure you don't have one that might be contra-indicated.

While you wait for the tea to steep in the bath (five minutes), consider letting go of the unbalanced expressions you've been experiencing and embrace the balanced aspects associated with each individual bath's focus. Ask your creator to amplify your intentions for healing these imbalances and to improve and increase your ability to let go of things you no longer need related to that. Release all the things that no longer serve you. Ask the gland or point of focus to accept the balance of this bath. Remember to stay in no longer than twenty minutes at the longest! Set a timer or bring in a clock so you can keep track, or ask someone to knock on the door to remind you to get out. Relax and enjoy your bath, focusing on your point and purpose.

A weekly bath is recommended for normally healthy people. Start with the bottom at the most physical vortex of the body (the Root) and work your way up to the most spiritual (the Crown), but if you feel like you need to do them in reverse order, that's okay too. Listen to your intuition about what's best for your personal situation. Your body may be trying to indicate to you the most out-of-balance one that needs the most attention right away.

First Vortex: Root

- Point: Spine and glandular system
- Unbalanced: Low self-esteem, self-centered
- Balanced: Stabilizing, grounded
- Color: Red
- Essential Oil: Vetiver, cypress, cedar wood
- Gemstone: Ruby, black tourmaline, red garnet
- Herbal Tea: Ginseng, dandelion root

Second Vortex: Sacral

- Point: Ovaries, testes
- Unbalanced: Overly sensitive, emotionally unbalanced, disempowered
- Balanced: Creative, balanced emotions, sexual flow
- Color: Orange
- Essential Oil: Jasmine, ylang ylang
- Gemstone: Orange carnelian, orange calcite aragonite
- Herbal Tea: Cinnamon bark

Third Vortex: Solar Plexus

- Point: Adrenals, pancreas
- Unbalanced: Fearful, judgmental
- Balanced: Strengthened personal power, raised self-esteem
- Color: Yellow
- Essential Oil: Ginger, geranium, helichrysum
- Gemstone: Pyrite, tiger's eye, citrine
- Herbal Tea: Ginger or mint

Fourth Vortex: Heart

- Point: Thymus gland
- Unbalanced: Possessive, fear of rejection
- Balanced: Love, unconditionally, voice of the soul, compassion
- Color: Green, pink
- Essential Oil: Rose, Melissa
- Gemstone: Rose quartz, jade, kunzite
- Herbal Tea: Licorice

Fifth Vortex: Throat

- Point: Parathyroid or thyroid gland
- Unbalanced: Unreliable, self-righteous
- Balanced: Satisfied, content, in your truth
- Color: Blue
- Essential Oil: Lavender or geranium
- Gemstone: Turquoise, blue calcite, aquamarine
- Herbal Tea: Lemon with turmeric

Sixth Vortex: Third Eye

Fountain of Water of Life

- Point: Pituitary gland
- Unbalanced: Undisciplined, highly logical
- Balanced: Brings focus, intuition, centeredness
- Color: Indigo
- Essential Oil: Sandalwood, clary sage
- Gemstone: Moonstone, sodalite, lapiz lazuli
- Herbal Tea: Schizandra berry, jasmine

Seventh Vortex: Crown

- Point: Pineal gland
- Unbalanced: Constantly exhausted, depressed
- Balanced: Soothes restless mind, higher awareness, prayerful
- Color: Violet
- Essential Oil: Frankincense, blue chamomile
- Gemstone: Amethyst, lepidolite, sugilite
- Herbal Tea: Astragalus root, lavender

For fun, here are some water proverbs for you to think about and see how many you've heard and know the true meaning and origins of the phrase. Find ways to use them in your conversations with people and see how many of them they've heard of!

Page 206

1. Blood is thicker than water.
2. To change mid-stream.
3. Don't throw the baby out with the bath water.
4. You can lead a horse to water but you can't make it drink.
5. When it rains, it pours.
6. A drop in the bucket.
7. Dry up your drip (that is, stop talking or gossiping, sharing too much information).
8. A fish out of water.
9. Get your feet wet.
10. Jump into the deep end.
11. Sink or swim.
12. In deep/hot water.
13. Make a big splash.
14. It's raining cats and dogs.
15. Still waters run deep.
16. Can talk under water.
17. The well has run dry.
18. To be under water, or: your head is under water.
19. To trouble/poison the water.
20. It's water under the bridge.
21. Watered down.
22. Wet behind the ears.
23. Wet your whistle.

If you would like to learn more about water, watch for our upcoming classes and workshops as well. Share what you have learned from this book with others around you who are also seeking to improve their wellness. Not only will it help you learn more, you will also add to and grow your support team.

On a final note, I want to talk with you about the word *redeem*. This one word carries a lot of power. It is divine and there is nothing else like it on earth. Merriam-Webster's Dictionary tells us the word *redeem* is a transitive word. Knowing what a transitive verb is, is very important to understand the word's full meaning.

A transitive verb tells us that a word like *redeem* has a relationship *to* the relationship with the property and the first element as well as a second one. It also holds true between the second and the third element. As well, it maintains the same relationship between the third element and the first. It has to do with a transition.

So to make it easier to understand, if you have three people named A, B, and C–: A is related to B. B is related to C. And C is related to A. Everything is related to each other. They're all related because of their interrelations.

   1. Redeem:
       a. To buy back: Repurchase.

    b. To get or win back.
2. To free from what distresses or harms, such as:
    a. To free from captivity by payment of ransom.
    b. To extricate [or, to take out] from or help to overcome something detrimental.
    c. To release from blame or debt: Clear.
    d. To free from the consequences of sin.
3. To change for the better: Reform.
4. Repair, restore.

Can you see where I'm going with this? All the pain and suffering we have lived through in our lives can be *gone*. Our experiences remain and the wisdom we've received stays with us. We don't have to walk in fear and turmoil the rest of our lives. That can completely – and I do mean *completely* – disappear. There is only one way it is possible for us to be able to do this, and that is through the fountain of living water.

The first definition of *redeem* is to buy back or to repurchase. We know what is done can possibly be undone under the right circumstances. This obvious one is that the Savior has paid a price to answer for and atone for our pain, sorrow, and more. He had to give something of great value for such damaging actions committed whether knowingly or ignorantly and for the burdens we've been carrying. And Christ has already done it for

Fountain of Water of Life

each and every one of us, whether we choose to accept the gift or not.

There is a *sweet* parable of the doughnuts I'd like to share with you on the following pages, and I hope you will experience the same joy and have some of the same realizations from it that I had.

Parable of the Doughnuts

A boy named John was attending school at a university where Mr. Christianson taught. The instructor had an open-door policy and would take in any student as long as they followed his rules. John had been kicked out of his sixth period and no other teacher wanted him, so he went to Mr. Christianson's class.

John was told he couldn't be late, so he would arrive just seconds before the bell rang, and he was always at the back of the room so he could be the first out the door when class was over. One day, Mr. Christianson asked John to stay after class so he could talk with him. After class he pulled John aside and said, "You think you're pretty tough, don't you?"

John's answer was, "Yeah, I do."

Then Mr. Christianson asked, "How many pushups can you do?"

John said, "I do almost two hundred every night."

"Two hundred? That's pretty good, John." Mr. Christianson said. "Do you think you could do *three* hundred?"

John replied "I don't know... I've never done three hundred at a time."

"Do you think you could?" asked Mr. Christianson.

"Well, I can try," said John.

"Can you do three hundred in sets of ten? I need you to do three hundred in sets of ten for this to work. Can you do it? I need you to tell me you can do it," Mr. Christianson said.

John said, "Well, I think I can... yeah, I can do it."

Mr. Christianson said, "Good! I need you to do this on Friday." Friday came, and John got to class early and sat in the front of the room. When class started, Mr. Christianson pulled out a big box of doughnuts. Now these were not the normal kinds of doughnuts. They were the extra fancy, *big* kind, with cream centers and frosting swirls. Everyone was excited it was Friday and, the last class of the day, and they were going to get an early start on the weekend.

Mr. Christianson went up to the first girl in the first row and asked "Cynthia, do you want a doughnut?"

Cynthia said "Yes!"

Mr. Christianson then turned to John and asked, "John, would you do ten pushups so that Cynthia can have a doughnut?"

John said, "Sure," and jumped down from his desk to do a quick ten.

Then John again sat at his desk. Brother Christianson put a doughnut on Cynthia's desk. Mr. Christianson went to Joe, the next person, and asked, "Joe, do *you* want a doughnut?"

Joe said, "Yes."

Mr. Christianson asked, "John, would you do ten pushups so Joe can have a doughnut?" John did the ten pushups, and Joe got a doughnut. And so it went, down the first aisle, 'til Mr. Christianson came to Scott.

Scott was captain of the football team and the center on the basketball team. He was very popular and never lacked for female companionship. When Mr. Christianson asked, "Scott, do you want a doughnut?" Scott's reply was "Well, can I do my own pushups?"

Mr. Christianson said, "No, John has to do them."

Then Scott said, "Well, I don't want one then."

Mr. Christianson then turned to John and asked, "John, would you do ten pushups so Scott can have a doughnut he doesn't want?"

John started to do ten pushups. Scott said, "*Hey*! I said I didn't want one!"

Mr. Christianson said, "Look, this is my class, desks, and my doughnuts. Just leave it on the desk if you don't want it." And he put a doughnut on Scott's desk.

Now, by this time, John had started to slow down a little. He just laid on the floor between sets because it took too much effort to get up and down. A little perspiration began coming out around his brow. Mr. Christianson started down the third row. The students were starting to get a little angry.

Mr. Christianson asked Jenny, "Jenny, do you want a doughnut?"

Jenny said, "No."

Then Mr. Christianson asked John, "John, would you do ten pushups so Jenny can have a doughnut she doesn't want?" John did ten, and Jenny got a doughnut.

By now, the students were beginning to say "No" more and more, and there were all these uneaten doughnuts on the desks. John was also having to really put forth a lot of effort to get these pushups done for each doughnut.

A small pool of sweat began to form on the floor beneath his face, and his arms and brow were beginning to get red because of the physical effort involved. Mr. Christianson asked Robert to watch John to make sure he did ten pushups in a set because he couldn't bear to watch all of John's work for all the uneaten doughnuts. So Robert began to watch John closely. Mr. Christianson started down the fourth row.

During his class, however, some students had wandered in and sat along the heaters located on the sides of the room. When Mr. Christianson realized this, he did a quick count and saw thirty-four students in the room. He started to worry if John would be able to make it.

Mr. Christianson went on to the next person, and the next. Near the end of that row, John was really having a rough time. He was taking a lot more time to complete each set.

John asked Mr. Christianson, "Do I have to make my nose touch on each one?"

Mr. Christianson thought for a moment and then said, "Well, they're your pushups... You can do them any way you want." And Mr. Christianson went on.

A few minutes later, Jason was at the door to the room and was about to come in when all the students yelled, "*No!* Don't come in! *Stay out!*"

Jason didn't know what was going on. John picked up his head and said, "No, let him come in."

Mr. Christianson said "You realize that if Jason comes in you will have to do ten pushups for him."

John said, "Yes, I understand. Let him come in."

Mr. Christianson said, "Okay, I'll let you get Jason's out of the way right now. Jason, do you want a doughnut?"

"Yes."

"John, will you do ten pushups so that Jason can have a doughnut?"

John did ten pushups very slowly with great effort. Jason, bewildered, was handed a doughnut and sat down.

Mr. Christianson finished the fourth row and then started among those seated on the heaters. John's arms were now shaking with each pushup in a struggle to lift himself against the force of gravity. Sweat dripped off of his face, and by this time, there was not a dry eye in the room.

The very last two girls in the room were cheerleaders and very popular. Mr. Christianson went to Linda, the second to last, and asked, "Linda, do you want a doughnut?"

Very sadly, Linda said, "No, thank you."

Mr. Christianson asked John, "John, would you do ten pushups so that Linda can have a doughnut she does not want?" Grunting from the effort, John did ten very slow pushups for Linda.

Then Mr. Christianson turned to the last girl, Susan. "Susan, do you want a doughnut?"

With tears flowing down her face, Susan asked, "Mr. Christianson, can I help him?"

Mr. Christianson, with tears in his own eyes, said, "No, he has to do it alone. John, would you do ten pushups so Susan can have a doughnut?"

As John very slowly finished his last pushup, with the understanding that he had accomplished all that was required of him, having done three hundred fifty pushups, his arms buckled beneath him, and he fell to the floor.

Then, Mr. Christianson turned to the room and said,

"This is how it was with our Savior Jesus Christ. He said to the Father, "Into thy hands I commend my spirit." [#] With the understanding that he had done everything that was required of him, Jesus collapsed on the cross and died – even for those people who didn't want his gift. And just like some of the in this room, many chose not to accept the gift that was provided to them."

~End~

How many times in our lives have we tried to hold onto our sorrow, pain, and grief? How often have we thought that we could do it alone? And how often have we had a chance to tidy these things up in our lives, and yet we don't *take* the chance? We may feel we don't need it or want it. We don't feel worthy of it. Or we want to try to do it ourselves without realizing we can't. The price has already been paid for us to have our doughnuts. He suffered for all our sickness, sorrow, and pain so *we* don't have to suffer them. We just have to be willing to give all that away to him and let him take it.

That's all there is to it. To let go of our pain, we have to first acknowledge it's there. We need to realize we need help. And we have to be willing to let it go and let something better take its place. There's a great comfort in that. The more you do it, the more you'll come to know it. As you let go of deeper pain, the more peace you'll feel, and the more joy and strength you'll get in your foundation.

It's all healing, no matter how you look at it. There's no shame in bandaging up a cut. Likewise, there's no shame in changing your mind about a behavior you no longer want to do in favor of a better one. This is where we come to the second definition of *redeem* which is: to free from what distresses or harms.

Fountain of Water of Life

What is causing that constant stress or strain in your life? Is it the past creeping up to shame you? Could it be the horror of things you experienced you can't seem to shake? Trying to press these unpleasant things down below the surface only works for us for a while. Over time it will require greater and greater effort to keep it submerged in the subconscious. As the years go by you will grow more and more tired from the constant strain. One day, like it or not, it will come up into your conscious mind. You can choose when and how that happens, with help, or it can come up all at once, out of control and messy.

SECTION 5
THE LAMP

YOU CAN DREAM of being free of harm, or you can choose to start the journey to liberate yourself today. Prepare for your own deliverance *now* so that you will be ready when God's timing comes together with your hard work and effort. Freedom from pain or freedom from the liberty of wellness, also known as sickness, are both your choices to make.

You must choose where you want to spend your energy. Often, we hold on so tightly that we don't know how to let go. We're afraid we will fall if we *do* let go, even if we know there's someone there who can grab our hand and help pull us up instead. You can't find a stronger, truer hand than that of the Savior. The closer you get to him, the more you learn his law and how it works and the more confident you become in him. He is unfailing.

We can look to him always. In spite of the results of our actions and choices, he will always be there to catch us and help us back up when we fall. Consequences must still come, and we should be grateful we have the chance to stand up and face them. It is the best way to forge our way to forgiveness and mending the things that have been broken.

When we speak of things that are broken, it is easy to imagine a lamp shattered in pieces on the floor. My mom always told us not to throw the ball in the house because we might knock something over and break it. We thought we could be careful

Page 223

enough not to, but she explained that accidents still happen no matter how careful you think you're being even as adults. We didn't really believe her, but told her we wouldn't do it anyway.

Once day, we didn't care enough to listen anymore because our game seemed more important to us in the moment. Mom ended up being right after all. The broken lamp was evidence of our disregard and disobedience. Her rule was meant to maintain a law or order in her home. It was intended to also save money in the family's budget. Due to changing trends, replacing the lamp was impossible, and she had really loved that lamp. It was my understanding also that there was something very special about the initial selection and acquisition of those specific lamps.

We had to carry the consequence of breaking the law until we could pay for replacing Mom's special lamp with a new one. In every penny we earned towards purchasing a new lamp, we witnessed the grief in our mother's eyes. Every evening when the other lamp was turned on to light the living room we felt the weight of the darkness where the first lamp used to sit. It was a nightly reminder of the need for us to make restitution.

An amazing thing happened, though, once we had made things right again. Mother's grief changed as she admired her new matching lamps.

(She kindly bought herself the second one that matched.) The darkness disappeared in the evenings too. The consequences of our unintended actions were also lifted with no more visible reminder of our error, and life was good again.

Once we had paid the price for our collective disobedience, we were able to change for the better. Of course, it would have been best for us if we'd never broken the lamp, in the first place, but we learned an invaluable lesson about playing with the ball or throwing anything else in the house. With our newly gained wisdom we were able to help our younger siblings understand the importance of following that particular rule. They benefited from our mistake and constant reminders, so they never had to pay that particular consequence.

We were so much happier having gone through our trial. For one, we had learned the value of forgiving and being forgiven. Another thing we learned was that even if we made a mistake, we could still do everything in our power to fix it. The third thing we learned was that the pain we went through ended up being worth it in the end. Not only did our mother end up getting to update her lamps to something she ended up loving just as much, but we learned that it's okay to make mistakes. It's okay to face painful things because they can end up coming out better in the end.

An important thing to note here is that we were given the opportunity to repair what was broken. Without this, we might have ended up down a long dark road of believing there can never be forgiveness – ever – for anything. We might have eventually given up on life itself. Even, we might have felt the need to punish ourselves forever for breaking the lamp. We could have been left feeling that we'd never be good enough to be loved again, never being able to do or be worthy of love and acceptance, not just to in relation to our mother but to everyone we would interact with over the course of the rest of our lives.

The most important thing to know is that no matter how broken inside you feel, whether by your own hand or the hand of another, there is hope. We can change *how* we *feel* about our pasts. We can't change circumstances that have already happened but we can remove ourselves from many of the consequences not of our making. We may wish mightily that we could.

We can do our best to rectify the consequences we've suffered or caused others to feel from our own actions and decisions. You may think your path has been set in stone. Since there's no changing the past, you may mistakenly feel like the only thing you can do is apologize with your words and keep moving on as if nothing happened. Sometimes words are enough to *start* repairing things for little offenses. But this does not restore anything and it's the big offenses that need to have a big, sincere show of restoration. Being excessive is a good thing in this situation.

Restore means to replace. "To bring back," according to definitions from Oxford Languages, "(a precious right, practice, custom, or situation), to reinstate." It means "to return (someone or something) to a former condition, place or position – repair or renovate (a building, work of art, vehicle, etc.) so as to return it to its original condition."

In the case of my mother's lamp, we could not restore it to its original condition. We were vacuuming tiny shards of glass out of the carpet for months afterwards. We could have said we were sorry and walked away, leaving our mother to pick up the pieces and pay the price for us. We could have easily let her pay for her own new lamps. I'm very grateful she did not allow us to do that. She would have done us a great disservice if she had.

Our mother taught us to save up and help not only clean up the broken pieces but to buy a new lamp to replace the lost one. A new pair of lamps to replace the set of lamps that had once matched was better than just replacing the one broken one.

We showed our mother not only through our words but also through our actions how very sorry we were. We also changed our hearts and our behavior not only by never throwing things in the house again after that, but we were also were anxiously engaged in reminding our younger siblings not to make the same mistake we had made. Mom could then see our apology was complete and sincere.

Some of us, even many of us, I suspect, have experienced things more difficult to deal with than merely a broken lamp. I'm not saying we were not extremely aggrieved by what we had done in that situation. We were. But some events have much longer lasting consequences. Some of these things take a lifetime or more to try to fix and restore. Undoubtedly one or more of these things have altered your life or maimed you either emotionally or physically – maybe even spiritually – for what seems like will be the rest of your life!

How could God let this happen, right? (God had nothing to do with it in the first place.) We can either hold onto our grievances to the point that they become lifetime grudges, or we can realize the emotional knife we are twisting is in our own hearts, and doing more damage to us than it could ever do to the one who originally harmed us. I know anger can feel like a constant companion as you try to understand what happened, how to get justice, and how or where to start looking to begin picking up all the little pieces that are left of your life.

Page 228

If we look just at the pure chemistry of holding onto anger, we will see that it creates acidity in the body. As our blood stream becomes overrun with the increase in acidic hormones, adrenaline from the fight or flight response, and the emotional blockages that the tension causes (creating a buildup of lactic acid), the more alkaline outer lining of our cells weaken. Some of the cells will begin to burst, releasing their acidic inner contents into the bloodstream. This, in turn, raises the acidity level even more, causing more cells to burst, and the process repeats. Long-term anger kills many cells in the body.

Another part of the body that is harmed by our anger is called a telomere, which is part of your DNA. This is confirmed by science. As the body becomes more acidic, whether from poor health habits or overriding anger or hatred, these protective ends become shredded. By hurting your own DNA your body cannot replicate the best version of you. However, by letting go of and working through our pain and sorrow rather than holding it in, we protect, and can rebuild our telomeres. We are restored and repaired.

If you've made it this far, you are in good company. Choosing to move forward with your own self-healing is important. More and more people are joining the revolution of good health. They are working on restoring their spirits. They are climbing their Mt. Everest's in life and rejoicing on the other side.

You can climb with us. We can work on it together. We have help from the other side of the veil. All we need to do is ask. Most people will not be ready or willing to take the journey with us. That's okay. The Lord works with us all on the best time table for each of us. He knows us well, and he knows the best way to win our hearts back to him when it's the right time.

Each and every one of us has to try to understand how to make our way back to him. It is not a simple task. It's different for each one of us. The general rules are the same, but the way they paint themselves out on each canvas can look completely different. It helps us to learn how to not judge others and not to cry when our hearts are hardened against them over the pain of their choices against us. It shouldn't matter the color of their skin or the size of their wallet or bank account. We can still show each other kindness and understanding.

When we rely on the One above to walk with us along the river of life, he can make more of us than we can do alone for ourselves. He will open the windows of heaven and pour out blessings on our heads, more than we could ever receive. He knows if we mean it. He won't just give it to us just because we ask. We have to work on it, through it, and for it. The work itself and what we gain from it is part of the blessing.

We have to fight for ourselves every day. Blessings come when we most need them. We may feel like we can't make it, that we're not strong enough to last through the process. Even when we're fainting, he holds us in the safety of his love, and he revives us to fight another day until we make it to the other side of life.

Real life and real living are the hope and dream we have. During our darkest hours, we hold to that image of the lives to which we want to be restored. We hope on it. We pray for it. Today we take action on it. We partake of the fountain of living water, the breath of life. We leave behind the desert of fear.

When we "walk uprightly" before God, he can pour his love into our hearts. It won't spill out. He fills our leaks and cracks until we are a perfect, complete vessel once again. Once we are full of his love, we can share that love with others. The water is so sweet and satisfying that you can't help but offer it to others and share *your* story with *them*.

Behind every crack of our brokenness, healing awaits. All we have to do is ask and then act. Healing does not happen only by asking alone. If we merely sit and ask, that's all we'll end up with.

We must ask and then act. We start with getting our spirits right; we start with hydrating our bodies and quenching our souls. We define every moment of our lives with joy and rejoicing. We *choose* to see it that way. Each sorrow offers us the opportunity to learn and grow from it. Each offense allows us the chance to heal and grow in power and strength.

We gain generosity, gratitude, strength, fortitude, knowledge, wisdom. We lose fear, incapability, anger, jealousy, envy, malice. We gain hope, helpfulness, harmony, and smiles! Sadness disappears more often, and sunshine shows its glorious rays in our life. We lose heartache and despair, hopelessness and rage. We have everything to gain and nothing broken to lose or that is even worth keeping when we join ourselves with the healing power of water and the healing power of Christ.

We sacrifice the things we don't need for everything we want to have in life. The joy of living, health, happiness, and love are some of the great things for which we hope. Restoration to all we once were (and now can be again) in life is something on which we wait. We don't have to sit around waiting for it to happen to us. The fountain of living water has already been paid for and is waiting for our partaking.

Will you come and partake? Like every good story, there is a beginning, middle, and an end. Your tale is no different. In order for there to be a journey, you have to *begin*. To reach the end, you have to keep going. One day you will reach the finish line but the part in the middle is what matters most after beginning. Come, drink of the fountain of living water.

"I am the door; by me if any man enter in, he shall be saved, and shall go in and out, and find pasture." [27]

This is one of the most beautifully intricate constructs known to man. It is so complex it boggles men's minds. Yet it is also so simplistic in nature, it is usually overlooked and dismissed by worldly eyes as a thing of naught. It's the perfect disguise! Misguided people would have you believe the concept of the gate and the pathway is hateful, filled with judgment, and full of wrath. Techniques, though misguided, and aimed at "fearing" and threatening people towards it by those who do not in reality understand its principles and end goal, realize a similar result as trying to herd a bunch of wild cats. Most will run away and a few will freeze up, unable to run but wanting to.

The Savior is the door to healing. The door to health, wellness, and happiness can only be entered by and through him. It cannot be entered to the left or to the right. You can't sneak in a back way. The only pathway to *light* is by him. Life is found *through* him. He has laid out the perfect twelve-step plan and given a true example in Christ of how to live it perfectly. And in spite of the men of the world seeking power, fame, and wealth by doing all they can to change it, hide it, and make it disappear altogether, the Savior's plan's rays of hopeful sunlight are breaking through *their* intended clouds of despair and hopelessness.

You may experience people challenging your activity of bathing, drinking pure, clean water, and partaking of the fountain of living water for your spiritual soul. In fact, you should *expect* it to happen and plan how you are going to respond to it in advance so you don't even have to think about it. You will be able to reply instantly and have a kind, informative response or consciously ignore the jabs and ridicule of your beliefs and healthy habits (much to their dismay).

The further in through the door you get and the more doorways you go through on the path and the more fully you live up to your covenants with God on the path to improving your health and happiness, the more safety you will feel in your life as you are protected from the harmful side-effects of others, and you will attract others to you who also have similar vibrational fields and a sense of integrity as you do. You will create an island of light and hope in your home, in your community, and in the world.

Enjoy the sweetness you have never yet known but always longed for. Find the peace your soul has roamed the world in search of. Come home to the place where you can feel you've always belonged and been loved and cared for. The journey begins within you, but you'll always go through him to get there.

As you come to know him, you'll begin to recognize that this is what you've been truly searching for. The homesick feeling will begin to fade, your burdens will become lighter, and the healing will transform you. How it looks will vary with each individual, but the steps and the pattern will be the same: drop by drop becoming a river of spirit, of healing, of peace.

The Fountain of Living Water!

~~~

Fountain of Water of Life

Bibliography

1: (Bible: The King James Version) Genesis (Gen.) 1:2 – And the earth was without form, and void; and darkness was upon the face of the deep. And the Spirit of God moved upon the face of the waters.

2: (KJV) Gen.1:7 – And God made the firmament, and divided the waters which were under the firmament from the waters which were above the firmament: and it was so.

3: (KJV) Gen. 1:9 – And God said, Let the waters under the heaven be gathered together unto one place, and let the dry land appear: and it was so.

4: (KJV) Exodus (Exo.) 7:20 – And Moses and Aaron did so, as the Lord commanded; and he lifted up the rod, and smote the waters that wee in the river, in the sight of Pharaoh, and in the sight of his servants; and all the waters that were in the river were turned to blood.

5: (KJV) Exo. 15:23 – And when they came to Marah, they could not drink of the waters of Marah, for they were bitter: therefore the name of it was called Marah.

6: (KJV) 2 Samuel (Sam.) 14:14 – For we must needs die, and are as water spilt on the ground, which cannot be gathered up again; neither doth God respect any person: yet doth he devise means, that his banished be not expelled from him.

7: (KJV) 1 Kings 22:27 – And say, Thus saith the king, Put this fellow in the prison, and feed him with bread of affliction and with water of affliction, until I come in peace.

8: (KJV) Job 14:19 – The waters wear the stones: thou washest away the things which grow out of the dust of the earth, and thou destroyest the hope of man.

9: (KJV) Isaiah (Isa.) 41:17 – When the poor and needy seek water, and there is none, and their tongue faileth for thirst, I the Lord will hear them, I the God of Israel will not forsake them.

10: (KJV) Isa. 43:2 – When thou passest through the waters, I will be with thee; and through the rivers, they shall not overflow thee: when thou walkest through the fire, thou shalt not be burned; neither shall the flame kindle upon thee.

11: (KJV) Isa. 55:1 – Ho, everyone that thirsteth, come ye to the waters, and he that hath no money; come ye, buy, and eat; yea, come, buy wine and milk without money and without price.

12: (KJV) Ezekiel 47:1 – Afterward, he brought me again unto the door of the house; and, behold, waters issued out from under the threshold of the house eastward: for the forefront of the house stood toward the east, and the waters came down from under from the right side of the house, at the south side of the altar.

13: (KJV) Acts 10:47 – Can any man forbid water, that these should not be baptized, which have received the Holy Ghost as well as we?

14: (KJV) Josh. 24:2 – And Joshua said unto all the people, Thus saith the Lord God of Israel, Your fathers dwelt on the other side of the flood in old time, even Terah, the father of Abraham, and the father of Nachor: and they served other gods.

15: (KJV) Genesis (Gen.) 6:7 – And the Lord said, I will destroy man whom I have created from the face of the earth; both man, and beast, and the creeping thing, and the fowls of the air; for it repenteth me that I have made them.

16: (KJV) Gen. 7:10 – And it came to pass after seven days, that the waters of the flood were upon the earth.

17: (KJV) Gen. 45:7 – And God sent me before you to preserve you a posterity in the earth, and to save your lives by a great deliverance.

18: (KJV) Exodus 14:30 – Thus the Lord saved Israel that day out of the hand of the Egyptians; and Israel saw the Egyptians dead upon the sea shore.

19: (KJV) Judges 7:7 – And the Lord said to Gideon, By the three hundred men that lapped will I save you, and deliver the Midianites into thine hand: and let all the other people go every man unto his place.

20: (KJV) 1 Chronicles 16:35 – And say ye, Save us, O God of our salvation, and gather us together, and deliver us from the heathen, that we may give thanks to thy holy name, and glory in thy praise.

21: (KJV) Psalms. 34:18 – The Lord is nigh unto them that are of a broken heart; and saveth such as be of a contrite spirit.

22: (KJV) Proverbs (Prov.) 20:22 – Say not thou, I will recompense evil; but wait on the Lord, and he shall save thee.

23. (KJV) Prov. 28:18 – Whoso walketh uprightly shall be saved: but he that is perverse in his ways shall fall at once.

24: (KJV) Luke 13:23 – Then said one unto him, Lord, are there few that be saved?

25: (KJV) Acts 2:40 – And with many other words did he testify and exhort, saying, Save yourselves from this untoward generation.

26: (KJV) Prov. 3:8 – It shall be health to thy navel, and marrow to thy bones.

27: (KJV) John 10:9 – I am the door: by me if any man enter in, he shall be save, and shall go in and out, and find pasture.

Additional Scriptures:

1. D&C 4:7 – Ask and ye shall receive; knock, and it shall be opened unto you. Amen.

2. (KJV) 1 Sam. 9:13 – As soon as ye be come into the city, ye shall straightway find him, before he go up to the high place to eat: for the people will not eat until he come, because he doth bless the sacrifice; and afterwards they eat that be bidden. Now therefore get you up; for about this time ye shall find him.

3. (KJV) 1 Sam. 23:1-5 – 1 – Then they told David, saying, Behold, the Philistines fight against Keilah, and they rob the threshing floors. 2. Therefore David enquired of the Lord, saying, Shall I go and smite these Philistines? And the Lord said unto David, Go, and smite the Philistines, and save Keilah. 3. And David's men said unto him, Behold, we are afraid here in Judah: how much more then if we come to Keilah against the armies of the philistines? 4. Then David enquired of the Lord yet again. And the Lord answered him and said, Arise, go down to Keilah; for I will deliver the Philistines into thine hand. 5. So David and his men went to Keilah, and fought with the Philistines, and brought away their cattle, and smote them with a great slaughter. So David saved the inhabitants of Keilah.

4. (KJV) 2 Sam. 2:1 – And it came to pass after this, that David enquired of the Lord, saying, Shall I go up into any of the cities of Judah? And the Lord said unto him, Go up. And David said, Whither shall I go up? And he said, Unto Hebron.

5. (KJV) 5:19-25 – 19. And David enquired of the Lord, saying, Shall I go up to the Philistines? wilt thou deliver them into mine hand? And the Lord said unto David, Go up: for I will doubtless deliver the Philistines into thine hand. 20. And David came to Baal-perazim, and David smote them there, and said, The Lord hath broken forth upon mine enemies before me, as the breach of waters. Therefore he called the name of that place Baal-perazim. 21. And there they left their images, and David and his men burned them. 22. And the Philistines came up yet again, and spread themselves in the valley of Rephaim. 23. And when David enquired of the Lord, he said, Thou shalt not go up; but fetch a compass behind them, and come upon them over against the mulberry trees. 24. And let it be, when thou hearest the sound of a going in the tops of the mulberry trees, that then thou shalt bestir thyself: for then shall the Lord go out before thee, to smite the host of the Philistines. 25. And David did so, as the Lord had commanded him; and smote the Philistines from Geba until thou come to Gazer.

6. (KJV) 2 Kg. 3:11-20 – But Jehoshaphat said, Is there not here a prophet of the Lord, that we may enquire of the Lord by him? And one of the King of Israel's servants answered and said, Here is Elisha the son of Shaphat, which poured water on the hands of Elijah. 12. And Jehoshaphat said, The word of the Lord is with him. So the king of Israel and Jehoshaphat and the king of Edom went down to him. 13. And Elisha said unto the king of Israel, What have I to do with thee? Get thee to the prophets of thy father, and to the prophets of thy

mother. And the king of Israel said unto him, Nay: for the Lord hath called these three kings together, to deliver them into the hand of Moab. 14. And Elisha said, As the Lord of hosts liveth, before whom I stand, surely, were it not that I regard the presence of Jehoshaphat the king of Judah, I would not look toward thee, nor see thee. 15. But now bring me a minstrel. And it came to pass, when the minstrel played, that the hand of the Lord came upon him. 16. And he said, Thus saith the Lord, Make this valley full of ditches. For thus saith the Lord, Ye shall not see wind, neither shall ye see rain; yet that valley shall be filled with water, that ye may drink, both ye, and your cattle, and your beasts. 18. And this is but a light thing in the sight of the Lord: he will deliver the Moabites also into your hand. 19. And ye shall smite every fenced city, and every choice city, and shall fell every good tree, and stop all wells of water, and mar every good piece of land with stones. 20. And it came to pass in the morning, when the meat offering was offered, that, behold, there came water by the way of Edom, and the country was filled with water.

7. (KJV) Luke 11:1-13 (here 1-4) – 1. And it came to pass, that, as he was praying in a certain place, when he ceased, one of his disciples said unto him, Lord, teach us to pray, as John also taught his disciples. 2. And he said unto them, When you pray, say, Our Father which art in heaven, Hallowed be thy name. Thy kingdom come. Thy will be done, as in heaven, so in earth. 3. Give us day by day our daily bread. 4. And forgive us our sins; for we also forgive every one that is indebted to us and let us not be led unto temptation; but deliver

Fountain of Water of Life

us from evil; for thine is the kingdom and power. Amen

8. (KJV) Luke 13:24 – Strive to enter in at the strait gate: for many, I say unto you, will seek to enter in, and shall not be able.

9. (KJV) 23:46 – And when Jesus had cried with a loud voice, he said, Father, into thy hands I commend my spirit: and having said thus, he gave up the ghost.

Additional Sources

1. *: Universal Pictures – (*The Prince of Egypt* (1998))

2. **: Hollywood, Charlton Heston, *The Ten Commandments* (1956)

3. ***: "The Route of the Exodus Journeys: Part I" Originally published in Ron's Newsletter #2 dated January 1993, accessed May 09, 2019 ronwyatt.com
https://www.ronwyatt.com/red_sea_crossing

4. ****: "When Trauma Gets Stuck in the Body: How do we heal?" Psychology Today, Posted October 23, 2019, accessed July 1, 2022, Psychologytoday.com
https://www.psychologytoday.com/us/blog/in-the-body/201910/when-trauma-gets-stuck-in-the-body

5. *****: "The Route of the Exodus Journeys: Part I" Originally published in Ron's Newsletter #2 dated January 1993, accessed May 09, 2019 ronwyatt.com
https://www.ronwyatt.com/red_sea_crossing

6. ++: "The Subsurface Imaging Project of Noah's Ark: The Results of the Subsurface Imaging Project of Noah's Ark", Website set up by John Larsen in 2017 to report on the results of the deep penetration resistivity scans of the remains of Noah's ark., http://noahsarkscans.nz/

Fountain of Water of Life

R. Shelton, NCLMT, BCTMB

R. Shelton is a licensed and board certified bodyworker, and has been hailed as an expert in the wellness industry. She specializes in clinical styled bodywork of many varieties. She is dedicated to results and living an example of wellness to her clients. She loves learning new things, cooking tasty recipes and eating them, dance, music, time with loved ones, and serving in her community.

Did you love the book? Thanks for writing a review! It helps me a lot in my and I really look forward to reading it. Best reviews are 150 – 200 words with new paragraphs every 2-3 sentences. You can mention how it personally helped you and how the book affected you. People love it.

Short on time? A review with stars helps too.

Typos: help us improve future editions by contacting us directly. We're very happy to fix them.

Also By/About:

Member Heal Thyself
Gripping life stories and instructional resources for modern day natural healing allowing the body's full potential.   https://memberhealthyself.com

Fountain of Living Water
Supplemental to 'Member Heal Thyself," this book covers the first resource *Hydration,* much more in depth including surprising details not included in the first book. Mysteries, inspiration, and personally tailored steps to try at home!

For: Corporate Wellness Plans, School/University, Class Resource Acquisitions, Book Clubs, Church Groups, Retail Stores, Addiction Recovery, etc...